YESHUA SPEAKS

The Paleo-Christian Teachings of Jesus for Nonbelievers

FIRST EDITION

YESHUA SPEAKS

The Paleo-Christian Teachings
of Jesus for Nonbelievers

FIRST EDITION

Stephen Snyder

Yeshua Speaks: *The Paleo-Christian Teachings of Jesus for Nonbelievers*

Gospel Passages used: *King James Authorized Version*, 1987 printing, by Public Domain. *The World English Bible*™ (WEB), by Public Domain.

Cover Design by LUGU. Luguwilmync.com

Turin Shroud Photograph by Secondo Pia.

Manuscript parchment: *Peshitta: Syrian Aramaic translation of the Bible*. Edessa Greece, 9th century. National Library, Givat Ram, Jerusalem.

Cataloging-in-Publication Data available from the Library of Congress on Request.

ISBN-13: 979-8-88940-354-8

YeshuaSpeaks.com

DEDICATION

For Ian and Virginia.

*Silver and gold have I none, but what I
have I give to you.*

Acts 3:6

And for my mother, who introduced
me to the essential teachings of Jesus.

CONTENTS

PREFACE

In 2009, a group of British atheists ran an advertising campaign that posted banners on city buses reading, "There probably is no god, now stop worrying and enjoy your life."

To me this typifies the profound, but unfortunately widespread, misunderstanding of the fundamental message of Jesus, which I hope you will find in the teachings that follow. Furthermore, I can safely say that most Christians do not spend much of their time burdened by the fear of an angry deity waiting to punish them someday.

Jesus primarily preached a vision of a God that loves and cares about you and wants you to have a better life, not a threatening message of condemnation and eternal damnation.

In brief, the converse of the atheist statement, "There is a God, so stop worrying and enjoy your life," is what lies at the heart of this book, and at the core of the teachings of Jesus. This positive sentiment is summarized nowhere better than in the first verses of the Gospel of Luke with the passage about the birth of Jesus:

Suddenly, there was with the angel a multitude of the heavenly army praising God, and saying, "Glory to

God in the highest, on earth peace, good will toward men." [1]

Who Is This Book For?

I have long felt there should be a simple, easy-to-read, and easy-to-understand book of Jesus' teachings for a secular audience. If you are curious about what lies at the heart of Christianity but don't really know where to start in a dizzying world of evangelical-centered self-help books, scholarly dissections of Bible passages, or incomprehensible and often frightening books about prophecy and apocalyptic end-times destruction.

This book is for nonbelievers, atheists, agnostics, followers of different faiths, and also disenchanted and disillusioned Christians whose church experience was overly negative or watered down by a focus on Old Testament or post-Gospel scriptures. This book is also for those who don't find much value in the rituals and traditions of churches and have only been introduced to the most rudimentary teachings of Jesus.

Without knowing the basic tenets of Jesus, you are at the mercy of the proponents, as well as the opponents, of Christianity to interpret for you what he said and what his movement is really about. In short, you can't truly know what to think about Christianity if you don't know what Christ said. I simply hope to expose non-Christians to the essential teachings of

---

[1] Luke 2:13-15

Jesus as they would have heard them preached by him 2,000 years ago.

Furthermore, and perhaps most importantly, I believe you don't have to abandon your heritage or culture to appreciate and draw value from the words of Jesus. There are Christians in every country of the world, and infinite ways within different ethnic and cultural traditions to follow Christ's teachings.

Indeed, much of protestant Christianity is based on a "personal relationship with Christ," so there can be as many unique forms of Christianity as there are Christians. I hope that you find some value in these teachings in your spiritual search for truth and they will help arm you against the misinformation you may receive from both sides of the debates about what Jesus preached and who he was.

Just as importantly, I hope this book reveals what Jesus did not say. My desire is that you can view Jesus with a new perspective and appreciate him for the revolutionary philosopher and teacher that we was, not a one-dimensional religious-historical figure so often caricatured by believers and nonbelievers alike.

My Qualifications

I am not a professional pastor, biblical scholar, academic, or theologian. I am not an ordained minister, I don't have a PhD in religious studies, and I don't speak ancient Greek or Latin. I am simply a follower of

and lifelong student of the teachings of Christ who became enamored by Jesus' teachings at an early age.
I was sent to a very conservative Christian school for several years and experienced much of the harshness and ungodliness that often drive people away from the church.

For me, this experience had the opposite effect and confirmed the truth of what Jesus said about the self-righteous, false prophets, blind guides, and those who block the door of the Kingdom by not going in themselves or letting others in.

I was determined that I was not going to let those false Christians drive me away from something so powerful and beautiful. My family also attended church at least three times a week, but I always felt that the power of the Bible lay in the words of Jesus, not in the admittedly supportive, but secondary, social, and cultural aspects of church attendance, rituals, and traditions.

Likewise, the writings of Paul and the other disciples of Christ or the Old Testament tales didn't have the same power and depth for me. Despite how comforting going to church was, it always seemed to me that the more challenging and often uncomfortable message of Jesus was largely ignored, with a preference given to post-Gospel writers such as the apostle Paul (apostle means "one who is sent off," "emissary, "or "messenger").

Similarly, although as a Christian I enjoy the powerful stories of Jesus' miracles and prophecies, death, and resurrection, and understand their importance, it seems clear that what Jesus taught is critically significant and often neglected.

There are certainly much more knowledgeable Bible scholars than me, and out of the estimated 2.38 billion Christians, I would certainly rank near the bottom in holiness and righteousness.

Nevertheless, all followers of Jesus are instructed to spread the Good News, so here is my humble attempt to share with you what has been such a positive influence on my spiritual journey, one which continues every day.

Finally, there is a line from the Bob Dylan song *Tangled Up In Blue* that best illustrates my experience studying the words of Jesus. It reads:

Then she opened up a book of poems
And handed it to me
Written by an Italian poet
From the thirteenth century
And every one of them words rang true
And glowed like burnin' coal
Pourin' off of every page
Like it was written in my soul from me to you [2]

---

[2]*Tangled Up In Blue* lyrics Copyright © 1974 by Ram's Horn Music; renewed 2002 by Ram's Horn Music. https://www.bobdylan.com/

9

That experience, unlike any I have encountered reading other spiritual or philosophical texts, is what I hope to share with you.

INTRODUCTION

Why is This Book Necessary?

The world, and America in particular, needs a spiritual revolution now more than ever. This fact seems to be increasingly evident even among those who are not spiritually minded. The world may in fact be on the verge of one, as William Strauss and Neil Howe predicted in their 1997 bestseller, *The Fourth Turning*.

There are hundreds of books produced each year about Jesus or living the Christian life by celebrity pastors or theologians. The problem with those books is that most of them are targeted at people who are already Christians who are looking for things that can further their spiritual journey, or students of theology who approach the phenomenon of Jesus with a detached intellectual curiosity.

What many of these books miss is that Jesus preached his message not only before the well-educated professional experts in the philosophy and religious teachings of the day, who largely rejected him, but to the outcasts, poor, illiterate, and misfits of society who accepted him in droves. In short, his message does not have to be conveyed by theologians, academics, or priests. That is why it is extremely important for you to read the New Testament for yourself, especially the foundation documents of the Gospels.

Unfortunately, there are few resources for non-Christians who have never been exposed to the actual words of Jesus and have the common perception of Christianity as fanatical, cultish, and narrow-minded without realizing that the teachings of Jesus are primarily an outcast's manifesto for the poor, the powerless, and those seeking spiritual enlightenment.

A Jesus for the Rest of Us
With the thousands of Christian books on the market that explore the divinity, Jewishness, miracles, message, history, or the historical life of Jesus, the world doesn't need another timid, meek, water-downed Jesus book or one that spends hundreds of pages dissecting a few selected passages or putting forth dense and convoluted theological theories.

For most of my life, I have been somewhat of a "Quiet Christian" not wanting to force my religious views on others, but I now feel that I need to speak out. I waited for many years for someone more qualified than myself to write a book for non-Christians on the teachings of Jesus, but I haven't seen one that speaks primarily to a nonbelieving or disaffected audience.

This book is for anyone who knows nothing of the teachings of Jesus or who has only heard the story of the life of Jesus, or the various debates surrounding the controversial aspects of Christianity, but not his actual words. This audience would, of course, be mostly those of you Muslims, Jews, Atheists, Hindus,

Agnostics, Buddhists, Sikhs, etc. who were not raised in a Christian church so had no exposure to the basic teachings of Jesus other than what you may have heard from mainstream sources.

This book is also for people nominally raised as Christians but who haven't spent much time exploring the roots of Jesus' teachings or whose church focuses primarily on ritual, tradition, post-Gospel writers, or Old Testament scriptures. That has been primarily my experience as a Christian and is a frustrating issue I hope can be rectified by a return to the basics of Christianity—Paleo-Christianity.

Why Reading the Teachings Is Vital
This book, and the teachings of Jesus in general, are meant as a lifelong guide for spiritual enlightenment, not just a collection of helpful sayings.

Perhaps most essential is that seeing for yourself what Jesus actually said you can protect yourself from those who would have you believing the Gospels say things they do not say or try to confuse you with a rapid-fire blizzard of quotes from Old Testament and post-Gospel writers to bolster their viewpoint. These come from Christians and non-Christians alike. Some of these assertions are well-intentioned and intellectually honest, some of them are not.

I will try to avoid getting lost in infinite debates or theological and academic terms most of us have never heard. I will avoid mind-numbing, overwrought theological concepts of Complementarianism, Antinomianism, Inerrancy, Immutability, Hypostasis, Hermeneutics, Chiliasm, Eschatology, Exegesis, Docetism, Ecclesiology, and a dizzying array of other theological concepts so far removed from Jesus' original teachings intended for the poor and uneducated.

Most people, even most Christians, often don't know or are not frequently reminded of what Jesus said. Most can probably hit the highlights such as "Love your neighbor," or "Do to others as you would have them do to you," but intentionally or not, most of our religious practice tends to bypass many of his more nuanced teachings intended to transform humanity and put us on a new spiritual path.

The bottom line is that you don't have to abandon your culture to gain value from the teachings of Jesus. You don't have to adopt the evangelical "praise and worship" culture, listen to Christian music, use the same catchphrases, dress or vote a certain way.

Jesus' teachings are simultaneously simple enough for children to grasp, but also infinitely able to provide spiritual insight and enlightenment over a lifetime. I hope these teachings will help you in your ongoing spiritual journey and help dispel any misunderstandings that may have turned you off from reading the actual teachings in the past.

A Jesus That Many Won't Recognize

Perhaps you have been told or have read things that have given what you think is an accurate representation of Jesus and his movement. Perhaps you have developed this perception of Jesus from popular television evangelists, political leaders, academics, and theologians, or conversely those vehemently opposed to Christianity or all religions.

Iconoclastic, revolutionary, and defiant, Jesus preached social justice, nonviolence, compassion, morality, ethics, and spiritual insight. His enigmatic teachings and parables require an individual to think and act—not rigidly follow the idolatry of tradition and ritual set forth by a priestly class. At its essence, Jesus' philosophy also focused on avoiding the many dead-end pitfalls of organized religion and freeing people from its burden.

How This Book Is Structured

The New Testament or Christian Bible is composed of only 27 books and roughly 300-400 pages, depending on the edition, compared to the Old Testament or Hebrew Bible, which has 39 books, not counting the Apocrypha, and roughly 950-1,000 pages. The teachings of Jesus, known as the Gospels or Good News, compose an even smaller part, just four books and around 150 pages. Furthermore, those four books contain many of the same passages which are often repeated by the four authors in slightly different forms.

So, you can see that the core teachings of Christianity are relatively concise.

I have divided the sayings into categories ranging from Anxiety to Wealth, with a separate section on what he said about religion. You may see that many teachings fit in multiple categories, but to avoid repetition, I have generally limited them to just one usage. I duplicate verses only where necessary.

The sayings are numbered not in order of importance or even in chronological order, but as a practical matter for reference, if you want to easily refer to them.

The old red-letter edition of the Bible with Christ's words highlighted I grew up with me as a child was helpful because I could zero in on just the words that Jesus spoke. I hope this book's format provides the same usefulness with a simple, easy to read and understand primer of Jesus' teachings.

The Name Jesus
Amid all the scholarly debates, even Jesus' name is complex. However, the current scholarship leans toward the opinion that *Yeshua* was the name he was given and is what he would have been called. However, current Aramaic Bibles and the Syriac Peshitta render the pronunciation *Yeshoo*.

The name Yeshua (Hebrew: יֵשׁוּעַ, Romanized: Yēšūaʻ) is a truncated late form of the early Hebrew name Yehoshua (Joshua) which was a common name during the Second Temple Period of the first century and is still in use today. The meaning of the name Yeshua is variably "Deliverer," "Yahweh brings salvation," or "God saves." The early Greek translation of Yeshua was *Iēsous*, which over the centuries evolved from the Latin *Iesus* into Jesus in the later western world.

The Son of Man
Jesus uses the sobriquet "Son of Man" several times to refer to himself. There are several meanings to this term ranging from the rather mundane equivalent of "a human" or "this guy," to the more significant son of man prophesied in the Hebrew Bible who would come to redeem God's people.

What's Not Included?
I haven't included the virgin birth, prophecies, and more mysterious things Jesus said, primarily found in the Gospel of John, or his miraculous healings or supernatural acts. This is not because I reject the divine nature of Jesus, but because I want to focus solely on the ethical teachings. I hope to explore those aspects of Christ's life and their meaning in a future volume.

I have also not included passages from the post-Gospel writers, which are primarily correspondence with the early churches. They are imminently valuable for further study but are supplemental, not equal, to the original teachings of Jesus, and are best understood in the context of having some knowledge of the Gospels.

Translations Used

With more than 60 English translations currently available online and in print I have chosen to use the *King James Version* (KJV) primarily with occasional alteration of words such as *thee* and *thou* to their modern equivalent. I also sometimes use passages from the *World English Bible*™ (WEB), an updated revision of the *American Standard Version*, with modern American English in places where it might make longer passages of the *KJV* more understandable for the modern reader.

I urge you to read the *KJV* and other versions of the New Testament in their entirety, most of which are available for free online, because they are truly beautiful translations for English speakers. You will also find many more surprising and enlightening aspects of Jesus' ministry, such as the supportive role of women and their prominence among his followers.

I also suggest reading the so-called Q Gospel, believed by contemporary scholars to be the original source for Matthew and Luke. Personally, I do not believe the first Gospel accounts were written down decades after Jesus lived as today's Bible scholars say, but much earlier, probably in Aramaic and are now lost to history. George Lamsa's work in ancient Aramaic and other clues point to this fact, but that's a topic for further study if you choose. I have put some resources in the Bibliography as a starting point.

Footnotes

Footnotes are added so you can compare the subtle variations between the four Gospel writers for the passages appearing in multiple books of the New Testament.

My Commentary

An in-depth study of the world of the Bible, its history, people, and culture are endlessly fascinating and worth studying for those of you so inclined. However, the teachings of Jesus generally stand on their own as universal truths, so I have tried to avoid excessive historical commentary.

In some instances, I have added a brief commentary in places where context and explanation might be needed to explain colloquial idioms of the time or historical characters or events. However, I often ask as many questions as I provide firm opinions. That is one of the fundamentals of this book. Seek guidance where you feel it is needed, but in your first reading let the spirit of these words guide you.

I've tried to use authoritative sources where necessary, but also my own opinion based on my own experience. So, don't accept my words on faith. Do your own examination. It is your journey.

Yeshua Speaks

The Word & The Way

The Essential Ethics & Philosophy

In the beginning was the Word, and the Word was with God, and the Word was God. The same was in the beginning with God. [3]

"The Word" as used in the Christian faith is a bit mysterious and like most of the scriptures has been hotly debated for the better part of 2,0000 years. It is believed by many to refer broadly to the Gospel message of Jesus. To many others, it is a more mystical and esoteric term with layers of meaning characteristic of the Gospel of John to refer to the second entity of the Holy Trinity who existed with God from the beginning of time.

Before it was known as Christianity, Jesus' movement was known as "The Way," likely stemming from Jesus' use of that phrase, but perhaps also from him saying, "I am the way, the truth, and the life." The Way suggests a journey, a path, and a direction to follow throughout life, as much as arriving at a defined location.

During his lifetime his appeal stretched from scholars to laborers, princes to peasants, men, women,

---

[3] John 1:1-2

and children. Early Christianity, also referred to as the Early Church or what I prefer, "Paleo-Christianity," is the first 300 years of the Christian movement. The first followers of Christianity were primarily Jews who had adopted the faith, but it quickly spread to Gentile communities in the Roman Empire.

Since the early days of the movement, Christians have commonly referred to Jesus as "Jesus Christ." Christ means "anointed one."

In the ancient Hebrew religion, oil was used to anoint the heads of important religious and political leaders. Anointed also referred particularly to the coming Messiah who would rescue the Israelites to establish and rule over an earthly kingdom for them.

According to the New Testament book of Acts[4], Antioch was where followers of Jesus were first called Christians. The first use of the term "Christianity" was around 100 AD by Ignatius Theophorus, an early Christian writer, and Patriarch of Antioch.

---

[4] Acts 11:26

THE TOP 20 TEACHINGS OF JESUS

If you don't have time to read this whole book, read these 20 verses. They sum up what I feel are the essential revolutionary philosophy and ethics of Jesus and the core of his Gospel or "The Good News."

1

Love God with all your heart, and with all your soul, and with all your mind. This is the first and great commandment, and the second is like it, love your neighbor as yourself.[5]

2

So, whatever you wish that people would do to you, do so to them; for this is the law and the prophets.[6]

---

[5] Matthew 22:37-39, Mark 12:29-31, Luke 10:27

[6] Matthew 7:12, Luke 6:31 ("The law and the prophets" refers to the core books of the Hebrew Bible (the Tanakh), the first five books (the Torah) and the Prophets.)

3

The Spirit of the Lord is upon me, because he has anointed me to preach good news to the poor. He has sent me to proclaim release to the prisoners and recovering of sight to the blind, to free those who are oppressed, to proclaim the year of the Lord's favor.[7]

4

I am come that they might have life, and that they might have it more abundantly.[8]

5

For the Son of Man is not come to destroy lives, but to save them.[9]

---

[7] Luke 4:18-19 (quoting Isaiah 61:1-2)
[8] John 10:10
[9] Luke 9:56

6

Truly, truly, I say to you, if anyone keeps my word, he will never see death. [10]

7

For God so loved the world, that he gave his only begotten Son, that whosoever believeth in him should not perish, but have everlasting life. For God sent not his Son into the world to condemn the world; but that the world through him might be saved. [11]

8

He that has two coats, let him give to him that has none, and he that has food, let him do likewise. [12]

---

[10] John 8:51
[11] John 3:16-17
[12] Luke 3:10

9

A new commandment I give to you, that you love one another; even as I have loved you, that you also love one another. By this all men will know that you are my disciples, if you have love for one another. [13]

10

Peace, I leave with you; my peace I give to you; not as the world gives do I give to you. Let not your hearts be troubled, neither let them be afraid. [14]

11

Truly, truly, I say to you, unless one is born anew, he cannot see the Kingdom of God. [15]

---

[13] John 13:33-35
[14] John 14:27
[15] John 3:3

12

I am the light of the world; he who follows me will not walk in darkness but will have the light of life. [16]

13

But love your enemies, and do good, and lend, expecting nothing in return; and your reward will be great, and you will be sons of the Most High; for he is kind to the ungrateful and the selfish. Be merciful, even as your Father is merciful. [17]

14

Blessed are they who hunger and thirst for righteousness: for they will be filled. [18]

---

[16] John 8:12
[17] Matthew 5:43-48, Luke 6:27, Luke 6:34-36
[18] Matthew 5:6

15

Not everyone who merely says to me, "Lord, Lord," will enter the Kingdom of Heaven, but he who does the will of my Father which is in heaven. [19]

16

Come to me, all who labor and are heavily laden, and I will give you rest. Take my yoke upon you and learn from me; for I am gentle and lowly in heart, and you will find rest for your souls. For my yoke is easy, and my burden is light. [20]

17

You judge according to the flesh, but I judge no one. [21]

---

[19] Matthew 7:21
[20] Matthew 11: 28-30
[21] John 8:15

18

For if you forgive people their transgressions against you, your heavenly Father will also forgive you. [22]

19

If you abide in my word, you are my disciples indeed. And you will know the truth, and the truth will make you free. [23]

20

If anyone would be first, he must be last of all and servant of all. [24]

---

[22] Matthew 6:14
[23] John 8:31-32
[24] Mark 9:35

ANXIETY & WORRY

Among the human concerns Jesus addressed were fear of death, guilt, loneliness, disconnection from your spiritual self, inner peace, and ethical and moral conduct, he also preached a message of freeing oneself from unnecessary anxiety.

He acknowledged that there were of course problems and troubles in this life, but to worry about things that haven't happened yet, or might never happen, was to limit the potential inherent in a positive and hopeful mindset. Even more limiting is to overly concern yourself with minor issues such as what clothes to wear or what food to eat.

The core principle here is there is a God, he loves you, and you don't have to worry about death. So, don't be consumed by the debilitating stress of physical concerns, and you will have a happier and more abundant spiritual life.

Teaching 1

Peace, I leave with you; my peace I give to you; not as the world gives do I give to you. Let not your hearts be troubled, neither let them be afraid. [25]

---

[25] John 14:27

Teaching 2

Aren't two sparrows sold for a penny and
not one of them will fall to the ground
without your Father knowing?

But the very hairs of your head are all
numbered. So, don't be afraid, you are of
more value than many sparrows. [26]

---

[26] Matthew 10:29-31

Teaching 3

Then Jesus was led up by the Spirit into the wilderness to be tempted by the devil. When he had fasted forty days and forty nights, he was hungry afterward. The adversary came and said to him, "If you are the Son of God, command that these stones become bread." But he answered,

It is written: "Man will not live by bread alone, but by every word that proceeds out of the mouth of God." [27]

---

[27] Matthew 4:1-4, Mark 1:13 Luke 4:1-4

Teaching 4

Therefore, take no thought, saying, What will we eat? or, What will we drink? or, how will we be clothed? For your heavenly Father knows that you need all these things.

But seek first the Kingdom of God, and his righteousness; and all these things will be given to you. So, don't worry about tomorrow: for tomorrow will worry about itself. Sufficient to the day is the evil thereof.

And he said to his disciples,

Therefore, I say to you, Take no thought for your life, what you will eat; neither for the body, what you will wear. The life is more than food, and the body is more than clothing.

Consider the ravens: for they neither sow nor reap, they neither have warehouse nor barn, and God feeds them. How much more are you more valuable than birds?

And which of you, by taking thought can add to his height one inch?

If you then are not able to do that thing which is least, why take you thought for the rest?

Consider the lilies, how they grow: they don't work, they don't make clothes; and

yet I say to you that Solomon in all his
glory was not dressed like one of these.
If then God so clothe the grass, which is
today in the field and tomorrow is cast into
the oven, how much more will he clothe you,
Oh you of little faith?

And seek you not what you will eat, or
what you will drink, neither be of a
doubting mind.

For all these things do the nations of the
world seeks, and your Father knows that
you need these things.

But rather seek the Kingdom of God, and
all these things will be given to you. Fear
not, little flock, for it is your Father's good
pleasure to give you the Kingdom.

Sell what you have and give to charity. Provide yourselves purses which don't grow old, a treasure in the heavens doesn't fail, where no thief steals, or moth destroys.

For where your treasure is, there will your heart be also. [28]

Studies confirm there is no relationship between wealth and happiness. After a certain level of income to take care of essential needs, wealth makes virtually no difference in overall welfare and contentment and, if anything, serves to diminish spiritual and ethical well-being.

---

[28] Matthew 6:25-34, Luke 12:22-28, Luke 12:29-31

Teaching 5

Truly, truly, I say to you, if anyone keeps my word, he will never see death. [29]

Jesus is speaking here of spiritual death in this life and in the next life.

---

[29] John 8:51

Teaching 6

Why are you so fearful? How is it that you have no faith?[30]

Teaching 7

Now it came to pass, as they went, Jesus entered a certain village; and a woman named Martha received him into her house. And she had a sister named Mary, who also sat at Jesus' feet and heard his Word. But Martha was burdened with much serving, and came to him and said, "Lord, do You not care that my sister has left me to serve alone? Ask her to help me." And Jesus answered and said to her,

Martha, Martha, you are anxious and troubled about many things.

But one thing is necessary, and Mary has chosen that good part, which will not be taken away from her. [31]

---

[31] Luke 10:38-42

Teaching 8

Let not your heart be troubled: you believe in God, believe also in me. [32]

---

[32] John 14:1

Teaching 9

Come to me, all who labor and are heavily laden, and I will give you rest. Take my yoke upon you and learn from me; for I am gentle and lowly in heart, and you will find rest for your souls. For my yoke is easy, and my burden is light.[33]

---

[33] Matthew 11: 28-30

THE BLESSED

Commonly known as "The Beatitudes," in Matthew this event is set on "a mountainside," so is often referred to as the Sermon on the Mount.

The Blessings recounted in Luke say it was on "a plain," which appears contradictory, but the Greek translation merely says, "on a level place."

These well-known teachings typify the beauty and simplicity of The Good News.

Teaching 10

And seeing the multitudes, he went up into a mountain: and when he was set, his disciples came to him. And he opened his mouth, and taught them, saying:

Blessed are the humble [34] for theirs is the Kingdom of Heaven. [35]

---

[34] Originally "Poor in Spirit" in the *KJV*.
[35] Matthew 5:3

Teaching 11

Blessed are the poor for theirs is the Kingdom of God. [36]

---

[36] Luke 6:20

Teaching 12

Blessed are they that mourn for they will be comforted. [37]

---

[37] Matthew 5:4

Teaching 13

Blessed are the gentle: for they will inherit the earth. [38]

---

[38] Matthew 5:5

Teaching 14

Blessed are they which hunger and thirst for righteousness: [39] for they will be filled. [40]

---

[39] i.e., Justice/integrity/morality.
[40] Matthew 5:6

Teaching 15

Blessed are the merciful: for they will obtain mercy. [41]

---

[41] Matthew 5:7

Teaching 16

Blessed are the pure in heart: for they will see God. [42]

---

[42] Matthew 5:8

Teaching 17

Blessed are the peacemakers: for they will be called the children of God. [43]

---

[43] Matthew 5:9

Teaching 18

Blessed are they which are persecuted for righteousness' sake: for theirs is the Kingdom of Heaven. [44]

Teaching 19

Blessed are you who hunger now,
for you will be filled.

Blessed are you who weep now,
for you will laugh. [45]

---

[45] Luke 6:21

CHARITY, GENEROSITY & SERVICE

Jesus says that you are not saved by good works because evil people can do good works for public praise (and today for tax credits), but by following his teachings, changing your thoughts, outlook, and behavior, i.e., being "born again." However, he says you will be judged by how you behave and treat your fellow human beings and this, along with sharing Jesus' teachings, should be the basis of any religious practice.

Teaching 20

Give, and it will be given to you: good measure, pressed down, shaken together, and running over, will be given to you. For with the same measure that you measure it will be measured back to you. [46]

---

[46] Luke 6:38

Teaching 21

He that has two coats, let him give to him that has none, and he that has food, let him do likewise. [47]

---

[47] Luke 3:10

Teaching 22

The Parable of the Sheep and the Goats

But when the Son of Man will come in his glory, and all the angels with him, then will he sit on the throne of his glory: and before him will be gathered all the nations: and he will separate them one from another, as the shepherd separates the sheep from the goats; and he will set the sheep on his right hand, but the goats on the left.

Then will the King say unto them on his right hand, Come, you blessed of my Father, inherit the kingdom prepared for you from the foundation of the world: for I was hungry, and you gave me to eat; I was thirsty, and you gave me drink; I was a stranger, and you took me in; naked, and you clothed me; I was sick, and you visited me; I was in prison, and you came unto me.

Then will the righteous answer him, saying, Lord, when saw we you hungry, and fed you? or athirst, and gave you drink? And when saw we you a stranger, and took you in? or naked, and clothed you? And when saw we you sick, or in prison, and came unto you?

And the King will answer and say unto them, Truly I say unto you, Inasmuch as you did it unto one of these my brethren, even these least, you did it unto me.

Then will he say also unto them on the left hand, Depart from me, you cursed, into the eternal fire which is prepared for the devil and his angels: for I was hungry, and you did not give me to eat; I was thirsty, and you gave me no drink; I was a stranger, and you took me not in; naked, and you clothed me not; sick, and in prison, and you visited me not.

Then will they also answer, saying, Lord, when saw we you hungry, or thirsty, or a stranger, or naked, or sick, or in prison, and did not minister unto you?

Then will he answer them, saying, Truly I say unto you, Inasmuch as you did it not unto one of these least, you did it not unto me. And these will go away into eternal

punishment: but the righteous into eternal life. [48]

I promised that I wouldn't focus too much on the afterlife because Jesus made it clear that humans don't understand their earthly life, much less a heavenly one, but this passage shows how seriously he takes the treatment of your fellow humans, and the consequences of our actions when we face God in the next life.

Jesus says God gives us spiritual gifts that we are to invest in doing good to our neighbors and translate into serving humanity based on what we have been taught by God. It is not enough to pursue spirituality for your own sake. We must put that knowledge to work on earth while we have time.

---

[48] Matthew 25:31–46

Teaching 23

And Jesus sat opposite the temple treasury and beheld how the people put money into the treasury and many who were rich put in much. And there came a certain poor widow, and she threw in two coins, which make a penny. And he called to him his disciples and said to them,

Truly I say to you, that this poor widow has put more in than all they that have put into the treasury; for they all put from of their abundance, but she from her poverty put in all that she had, even all her savings.[49]

---

[49] Mark 12:41-44

Teaching 24

You are the light of the world. A city located on a hill can't be hidden.

Neither do you light a lamp and put it under a measuring basket, but on a stand; and it shines to all who are in the house.

Even so, let your light shine before men, that they may see your good works and glorify your Father who is in heaven. [50]

---

[50] Matthew 5:14-16

Teaching 25

Give to everyone that asks of you, and of him that takes away your goods, ask them not back. [51]

---

[51] Luke 6:30

Teaching 26

Whoever compels you to go one mile, go
with him two. Give to him who asks you,
and don't turn away him who desires to
borrow from you. [52]

Roman soldiers were allowed to compel the local
civilian population traveling the roads with them to
carry their baggage for one mile. This teaching is
recognizable in the modern vernacular as "going the
extra mile," and stresses that the role of anyone seeking
God is of a humble servant of humankind, both
physically and spiritually who gives more than is
expected or required.

---

[52] Matthew 5:41-42

Teaching 27

When you give a dinner or a banquet, do
not invite your friends or your brothers or
your kinsmen or rich neighbors, so that
they also invite you in return, and you be
repaid.

But when you give a feast, invite the poor,
the maimed, the lame, the blind, and you will
be blessed, because they cannot repay
you. You will be repaid at the resurrection
of the just. [53]

---

[53] Luke 14:12-14

Teaching 28

Whoever gives one of these little ones just a cup of cold water to drink in the name of a disciple, most certainly I tell you, he will in no way lose his reward. [54]

---

[54] Matthew 10:42

Teaching 29

If anyone would be first, he must be last of all and servant of all. [55]

---

[55] Mark 9:35

Teaching 30

Yet lack you one thing: sell all that you have, and distribute to the poor, and you will have treasure in heaven: and come, follow me. [56]

---

[56] Luke 18:22

Teaching 31

For the Son of Man will come in the glory of his Father with his angels, and then he will render to everyone according to his deeds. [57]

---

[57] Matthew 16:27

DISCIPLESHIP

In these passages, Jesus gives us a guide for true discipleship, asking to be followed, not worshipped, and that behavior toward others is inextricably linked with discipleship.

Jesus also makes clear that all those who do the will of God are his followers. This makes things a bit more complicated for those who draw sharp boundaries around Christianity and those who go to Heaven.

You don't have to adopt the culture of any particular church or its prescribed rituals. I'm not knocking any form of practicing Christianity. I am a firm believer in freedom of religion and freedom of practice, as well as the old saying that "It takes all kinds." Churches do provide valuable growth, social support, and learning opportunities, but you must maintain your own discernment, intellect, and individuality or you could easily fall prey to cultlike thinking.

My point is that you can grow your own form of discipleship following Jesus' teachings with as much or as little influence from others as you wish.

Teaching 32

Not everyone who merely says to me, "Lord, Lord," will enter the Kingdom of Heaven, but he who does the will of my Father which is in heaven. [58]

Teaching 33

I tell you that many will come from the east and the west, and will sit down with Abraham, Isaac, and Jacob in the Kingdom of Heaven, but the children of the Kingdom will be thrown out into the outer darkness. There will be weeping and gnashing of teeth." [59]

The "children of the Kingdom" here are those who were claiming ownership of God as the exclusive children of Abraham.

---

[59] Matthew 8:11-12

Teaching 34

If you abide in my word, you are my disciples indeed. And you will know the truth, and the truth will make you free. [60]

---

[60] John 8:31-32

Teaching 35

Come to me, all who labor and are heavily laden, and I will give you rest. Take my yoke upon you and learn from me; for I am gentle and lowly in heart, and you will find rest for your souls. For my yoke is easy, and my burden is light. [61]

Jesus didn't come with a new set of strict rules and regulations, complicated dogma, or theatrical liturgy governed by a hierarchy of priests. In many ways, he was offering freedom from the burdens of all the religions that existed before.

---

[61] Matthew 11:28-30

Teaching 36

While Jesus talked to the people his mother and his brothers stood outside, eager to speak with him. Then one said to him, "Behold, your mother and your brothers stand outside, wanting to speak with you." But he answered and said to him that told him,

Who is my mother? And who are my brothers?

And he stretched forth his hand toward his disciples, and said,

Behold my mother and my brothers! For whoever will do the will of my Father who is in heaven, the same is my brother, and sister, and mother. [62]

---

[62] Matthew 12:46-50

Teaching 37

Everyone who has left houses, or
brothers, or sisters, or father, or mother, or
wife, or children, or lands, for my name's
sake, will receive one hundred times, and
will inherit eternal life. [63]

Jesus offers yet another example of something that
leads to reward from God as well as to eternal life—
adherence to his mission of serving humanity and
preaching a message of love and peace.

---

[63] Matthew 19:29

Teaching 38

If a man loves me, he will keep my word, and my Father will love him, and we will come to him and make our home with him.

He who does not love me does not keep my words, and the word which you hear is not mine but the Father who sent me. [64]

---

[64] John 14:23-24

Teaching 39

Whoever does the will of God my Father
is my brother, and sister, and mother. [65]

---

[65] Matthew 16:25, Mark 3:35

Teaching 40

You know that the rulers of the Gentiles lord it over them, and their great men exercise authority over them.

It will not be so among you, but whoever would be great among you must be your servant, and whoever would be first among you must be your slave; even as the Son of Man came not to be served but to serve, and to give his life as a ransom for many. [66]

---

[66] Matthew 20: 25-28

Teaching 41

No longer do I call you servants, for a servant does not know what his master is doing; but I have called you friends, for all things that I heard from my Father I have made known to you. [67]

This stunningly revolutionary statement upsets any notion of a church built on hierarchy or top-down leadership. If Jesus is calling his disciples friends, not servants, not to mention the post-Gospel pronouncement in Galatians that there is no difference between Jew and Gentile or even between men in women in this new movement, then where is the basis for a rigidly structured church?

---

[67] John 15:15

Teaching 42

I am the bread of life; he who comes to me
will not hunger, and he who believes in me
will never thirst. [68]

---

[68] John 6:35

Teaching 43

If anyone thirsts, let him come to me and drink. He who believes in me, as the scripture has said, "Out of his heart will flow rivers of living water." [69]

---

[69] John 7:37-38

Teaching 44

And if you salute your friends only, what do you do more than others? Do not even the publicans[70] do so?

Be therefore perfect, even as your Father who is in heaven is perfect.[71]

---

[70] Publicans were corrupt tax collectors for the Romans who often embezzled from the public funds they collected.
[71] Matthew 5:47-48

Teaching 45

All authority in heaven and on earth has been given to me. Therefore, go and make disciples of all nations, baptizing them in the name of the Father, Son, and the Holy Spirit, and teaching them to obey everything I have commanded you.

And surely, I am with you always, to the very end of the age. [72]

---

[72] Matthew 28:16-20

Teaching 46

The Parable of the Wise and Foolish Builders

Therefore, whoever hears these sayings of mine, and doeth them, I will liken him to a wise man, which built his house upon a rock:

And the rain descended, and the floods came, and the winds blew, and beat upon that house; and it fell not: for it was founded upon a rock.

And every one that hears these sayings of mine, and doeth them not, will be likened to a foolish man, which built his house upon the sand:

And the rain descended, and the floods came, and the winds blew, and beat upon that house; and it fell: and great was the fall of it.

And it came to pass, when Jesus had ended these sayings, the people were astonished at his doctrine: For he taught them as one having authority, and not as the scribes. [73]

---

[73] Matthew 7:24-29

Teaching 47

Truly, truly, I say to you, you will weep and lament, but the world will rejoice; you will be sorrowful, but your sorrow will turn into joy.

When a woman is in labor, she has sorrow, because her hour has come; but when she is delivered of the child, she no longer remembers the anguish, for joy that a child is born into the world.

So, you have sorrow now, but I will see you again and your hearts will rejoice, and no one will take your joy from you.[74]

---

[74] John 16:20-22

Teaching 48

Now great multitudes were going with him. Jesus turned and said to them,

If anyone comes to me, and doesn't disregard his own father, mother, wife, children, brothers, and sisters, yes, and his own life also, he can't be my disciple.

Whoever doesn't bear his own cross, and come after me, can't be my disciple.

For which of you, desiring to build a tower, doesn't first sit down and count the cost, to see if he has enough to complete it?

Or perhaps, when he has laid a foundation, and is not able to finish, everyone who sees begins to mock him, saying, "This man began to build and wasn't able to finish."

Or what king, as he goes to encounter another king in war, will not sit down first and consider whether he is able with ten thousand to meet him who comes against him with twenty thousand?

Or else, while the other is yet a great way off, he sends an envoy, and asks for conditions of peace.

So therefore, whoever of you doesn't renounce all that he has, he can't be my disciple.

$\bigcirc$alt is good, but if the salt becomes flat and tasteless, what do you season it?

It is fit neither for the soil nor for the manure pile. It is thrown out. He who has ears to hear, let him hear. [75]

Skeptics think the call above to "take up your cross and follow me," as it says in the KJV, is a much too prescient foreshadowing of Jesus' crucifixion, and therefore casts doubt on the authenticity of this passage, and by extension, calls into question the veracity of the Gospels as a whole.

However, in approximately 100 BC the Roman General and Consul Marius instituted reforms to the Roman Army reducing the size of the baggage train by having Legionnaires carry more of their own equipment to increase the speed and agility of the troops (and probably to reduce the cost to the government). The result was that Roman soldiers now were required to carry a massive 60–70-pound marching pack on a wooden cross-shaped frame called a "furca," which was so overloaded with tools,

---

[75] Matthew 16:24, Luke 14:25-35

weapons, and supplies that they were mockingly called "Marius's mules."

Jesus may have literally called his would-be disciples to sacrifice their material life, pack their bags, and follow him, potentially facing persecution and death, or to bring all their earthly spiritual burdens as they follow his teachings, or both.

The lesson here is that if you are skeptical of what Christian texts say, it is wise to be skeptical of what the expert detractors say as well. The truth is not always lying on the surface for all to see.

Teaching 49

He that loves his life will lose it; and he that
hates his life in this world will keep it unto
life eternal.

If any man serve me, let him follow me; and
where I am, there will also my servant be: if
any man serve me, him will my Father
honor. [76]

---

[76] John 12:25-26

Teaching 50

John answered, "Master, we saw someone casting out demons in your name, and we forbade him, because he doesn't follow with us."

Jesus said to him,

Don't forbid him, for he who is not against us is for us. [77]

Mark's version has Jesus saying, "Forbid him not: for there is no man which will do a miracle in my name, that can lightly speak evil of me." This provides a cautionary tale for Christians who would be tempted to reject as "true Christians" anyone who doesn't belong to their own group or follow their practices and scripture interpretations.

---

[77] Mark 9:38-39, Luke 9:49-50

Teaching 51

Blessed are they which are persecuted for righteousness' sake: for theirs is the Kingdom of Heaven.

Blessed are you, when men will revile you, and persecute you, and will say all manner of evil against you falsely, for my sake.

Rejoice, and be exceedingly glad: for great is your reward in heaven: for so persecuted they the prophets which were before you.[78]

---

[78] Matthew 5:10-12

ETHICS

Universally respected, even among non-believers and theological opponents of Christianity, the moral code of Jesus constitutes not just a rebuke of human moral failings but also an inspiring, but totally attainable, vision of the ethics to which we can all aspire.

Teaching 52

As you would like people to do to you, do the same to them. [79]

---

[79] Matthew 7:12, Luke 6:31

Teaching 53

Then also came publicans[80] to be baptized, and said to him, "Master, what will we do?" and he said to them,

Charge no more than that which is appointed you.[81]

And the soldiers likewise demanded of him, saying, And what will we do? And he said to them,

Do violence to no man, neither accuse any falsely; and be content with your wages.[82]

This could be one of the most challenging commandments when Jesus tells a soldier to do violence to no man. As an occupying army, the

Romans had a reputation for being physically abusive to the local population. But there is a broader philosophy implied here. There is no promotion of just war and certainly no allowance for preemptive military aggression against other nations. Jesus doesn't say to the audience, "You must perform certain religious rites or swear to profess a religious code of beliefs," when asked what to do by the audience. This passage also illustrates that Jesus had a mixed audience—not just Galileans and Judeans.

Jesus had a vast following beyond the twelve core apostles, many of whom seem to have been largely unknown to the apostles and who independently spread Jesus' words. His audience would have been strict observant Judeans, Hellenized Jews, Roman citizens, Samaritans, Galilean Jews, and any of the host of other people of varying nationalities and religions living or traveling in the bustling region from Syria down to Egypt and stretching from the Mediterranean across the Jordan river.

Palestine was an important cultural and trade crossroads of the Roman Empire and it's clear from these verses that a wide group of people was attracted to Jesus. Clearly, he set the Galilean/Judean Israelite people as his primary audience but always followed on quickly that the Gentiles from all over the world would be given an equal share of the Kingdom.

Teaching 54

You have heard that it has been said, You will love your neighbor, and hate your enemy. But I say to you, Love your enemies, bless them that curse you, do good to them that hate you, and pray for them which spitefully use you, and persecute you;

That you may be the children of your Father which is in heaven: for he makes his sun to rise on the evil and on the good and sends rain on the just and on the unjust.

For if you love them which love you, what reward have you? Do not even the publicans the same?

And if you salute your brethren only, what do you more than others? Do not even the publicans so? Be you therefore perfect, even as your Father who is in heaven is perfect.

And if you lend to those from whom you hope to receive, what credit is that to you? Even sinners lend to sinners, to receive as much again.

But love your enemies, and do good, and lend, expecting nothing in return; and your reward will be great, and you will be sons of the Most High; for he is kind to the ungrateful and the selfish. Be merciful, even as your Father is merciful. [83]

---

[83] Matthew 5:43-48, Luke 6:27, Luke 6:34-36

Teaching 55

Pharisees came to him, testing him and saying, "Is it lawful for a man to divorce his wife for any reason?" He answered,

Haven't you read that he who made them from the beginning made them male and female, and said, "For this cause a man shall leave his father and mother, and shall be joined to his wife; and the two shall become one flesh?"

So that they are no more two, but one flesh. What therefore God has joined together, don't let man tear apart.

They asked him, "Why then did Moses command us to give her a certificate of

divorce and divorce her?" He said to
them,

Moses, because of the hardness of your
hearts, allowed you to divorce your wives,
but from the beginning it has not been so.

I tell you that whoever divorces his wife,
except for adultery, and marries another,
commits adultery; and he who marries her
when she is separated from her husband
commits adultery. [84]

The important part of this question from the Pharisees
is "for any reason." In Jesus' world, women were
extremely vulnerable in society, and their lives were at
the whim of men, especially in marriage. A husband
could divorce his wife for the most trivial of reasons
and leave her homeless, penniless, and destitute for
such minor offenses as ruining dinner.

---

[84] Matthew 19:3-9, Matthew 5:31-32, Mark 10:2-12, Luke 16:18

Jesus speaks to the hardness of their hearts and reminds them that the original law of Moses allowed divorce for adultery only—and more broadly that you should not be immoral and cold-hearted, but these laws are only created out of necessity to give some measure of protection for the weaker party.

In the book of Luke, divorce is translated as "put away," which some scholars interpret as meaning that unless a man has given his wife a properly recognized order of divorce, he is committing adultery if he marries someone else, and if he marries a woman who has been put out by her husband without a proper divorce, he is also committing adultery.

Teaching 56

You have heard that it was said by them of old time, You will not kill; and whoever will kill will be in danger of the judgment:

But I say to you, That whoever is angry with his brother without a cause will be in danger of the judgment: and whoever will say to his brother, "Raca," will be in danger of the council: but whoever will say, "You fool," will be in danger of hell fire.

Therefore, if you bring your gift to the altar, and there remember that your brother has anything against you.

Leave there your gift before the altar and go your way; first be reconciled to your brother, and then come and offer your gift.

Agree with your adversary quickly, whiles you are in the way with him; lest at any time the adversary deliver you to the judge, and the judge deliver you to the officer, and you be cast into prison.

Truly I say to you, You will by no means come out thence, till you hast paid the uttermost penny. [85]

Raca is an insult derived from an Aramaic word meaning empty-headed or stupid. George M. Lamsa's Aramaic translation [86] says that *Raca* means, "I spit on you," and the word *fool* in the same verse translates more accurately to *effeminate*. Either way, Jesus

[85] Matthew 5:21-26
[86] *Holy Bible From the Ancient Eastern Text*, Harper San Franciso, 1985.

strongly admonishes the use of hurtful personal insults, especially ones regarding one's sexuality, which were rampant at the time among competing religious groups and in the culture more broadly.

FAITH & BELIEF

The word faith is perhaps the most used word in modern Christianity. Trust might be a better term. Jesus does not talk about belief in imaginary invisible things of which you have no evidence as many anti-religious detractors suggest, but about trust in your own power as well as God's power to do great things.

I have not included all of the instances where Jesus speaks of faith in the Gospels because many are associated with miracles and the role of faith in them. Without a doubt, miracles and mysterious esoteric sayings of Jesus are so intertwined with his ethical teachings they can be difficult to separate. God willing, I will cover those important teachings in a future volume, but I have included a few here to show the role of faith is not just believing something will happen, but that trusting makes it happen.

Jesus makes clear that the beneficiaries of these miracles are often active participants in them. This concept goes beyond "faith healing" and the placebo effect. Jesus says time and again that God has given humans immense spiritual power that we invariably underestimate and underutilize because of self-doubt.

Teaching 57

Now on his way to Jerusalem, Jesus traveled along the border between Samaria and Galilee. As he was going into a village, ten men who had leprosy met him.

They stood at a distance and called out in a loud voice, "Jesus, Master, have pity on us!" When he saw them, he said,

Go, show yourselves to the priests.

And as they went, they were cleansed.

One of them, when he saw he was healed, came back, praising God in a loud voice. He threw himself at Jesus' feet and thanked him—and he was a Samaritan. Jesus asked,

Were not all ten cleansed? Where are the other nine? Has no one returned to give praise to God except this foreigner?

Then he said to him,

Rise and go; your faith has made you well. [87]

Like many of the stories of miracles in the Gospels, the core lesson here is not about the healing itself but the beneficiary's role in achieving it. Amazingly, Jesus does not take credit for healing the man, but instead credits God and the man's own belief.

Perhaps even more important is the depiction of human nature. It is also important to see the lesson that ten men were healed but only one said thank you. And he was a Samaritan, a despised group not considered true Jews by the Judeans.

---

[87] Luke 17:11-19

Teaching 58

If you can believe, all things are possible to him that believes. [88]

Jesus repeats this concept several times, promoting the idea that we all have tremendous power within ourselves to heal and do great things if we believe we can. This might be considered the original law of attraction now popularized in books such as The Secret.

Unfortunately, this beautiful and empowering concept has been coopted by New Age gurus whose focus is often on financial prosperity and quasi-occult beliefs.

What Jesus taught was that faith is not just the belief that something good will happen but that your faith can make them happen. As always, he emphasized looking for spiritual miracles and blessings, not material ones.

---

[88] Mark 9:23

Teaching 59

When he came into Capernaum, a centurion came to him, asking him for help, saying, "Lord, my servant lies in the house paralyzed, grievously tormented." Jesus said to him,

I will come and heal him.

The centurion answered, "Lord, I'm not worthy for you to come under my roof. Just say the word, and my servant will be healed. For I am also a man under authority, having under myself soldiers. I tell this one, 'Go,' and he goes; and tell another, 'Come,' and he comes; and tell my servant, 'Do this,' and he does it."

When Jesus heard it, he marveled and said to those who followed,

Most certainly I tell you, I haven't found so
great a faith, not even in Israel.

Jesus said to the centurion,

Go your way. Let it be done for you
because you believed. [89]

---

[89] Matthew 8:5-10, 13

Teaching 60

Then the disciples came to Jesus privately, and said, "Why weren't we able to cast the demon out?"

He said to them,

Because of your unbelief. For most certainly I tell you, if you have faith as a grain of mustard seed, you will tell this mountain,

"Move from here to there," and it will move; and nothing will be impossible for you.[90]

Matthew 17:19-20

Teaching 61

Jesus answered them,

Most certainly I tell you, if you have faith and don't doubt, you will not only do what was done to the fig tree, but even if you told this mountain, "Be taken up and cast into the sea," it would be done. [91]

---

[91] Matthew 21:21

Teaching 62

Jesus answered them,

Have faith in God. For most certainly I tell you, whoever may tell this mountain, "Be taken up and cast into the sea," and doesn't doubt in his heart, but believes that what he says is happening; he shall have whatever he says.

Therefore, I tell you, all things whatever you pray and ask for, believe that you have received them, and you shall have them. [92]

---

[92] Mark 11:22-24

Teaching 63

Seeing their faith, he said to him,

Man, your sins are forgiven you.[93]

---

[93] Luke 5:20

Teaching 64

He said to the woman,

Your faith has saved you. Go in peace. [94]

---

[94] Luke 7:50

FORGIVENESS

In the following scriptures, Jesus describes an ongoing, continual process of redemption and forgiveness that involves you, your fellow humans, and God. How God judges you is directly based on your behavior toward others.

Your forgiveness is not a one-time action after which you're set for life, as is often taught by the self-centered doctrines that end with personal salvation, and after which there is an escape from personal responsibility or God's judgment.

Teaching 65

Judge not, and you will not be judged:
condemn not, and you will not be
condemned: forgive, and you will be
forgiven:

Give, and it will be given to you; good
measure, pressed down, and shaken
together, and running over, will men give
into your bosom.

For with the same measure that you
measure it will be measured to you again.[95]

---

[95] Matthew 7:1-2, Luke 6:37-38

Teaching 66

The Parable of the Two Debtors

One of the Pharisees invited him to eat with him. He entered the Pharisee's house and sat at the table. Behold, a woman in the city who was a sinner, when she knew that he was reclining in the Pharisee's house, brought an alabaster jar of ointment.

Standing behind at his feet weeping, she began to wet his feet with her tears, and she wiped them with the hair of her head, kissed his feet, and anointed them with the ointment. Now when the Pharisee who had invited him saw it, he said to himself, "This man, if he were a prophet, would have perceived who and what kind of woman this is who touches him, that she is a sinner." Jesus answered him,

Simon, I have something to tell you.

He said, "Teacher, say on."

A certain lender had two debtors. The one owed five hundred denarii, and the other fifty. When they couldn't pay, he forgave them both. Which of them therefore will love him most?

Simon answered, "He, I suppose to whom he forgave the most." He said to him,

You have judged correctly."

Turning to the woman, he said to Simon,

Do you see this woman? I entered your house, and you gave me no water for my feet, but she wet my feet with her tears, and wiped them with the hair of her head.

You gave me no kiss, but she, since the time I came in, has not ceased to kiss my feet. You didn't anoint my head with oil, but she has anointed my feet with ointment.

Therefore, I tell you, her sins, which are many, are forgiven, for she loved much. But one to whom little is forgiven, loves little."

He said to her,

Your sins are forgiven. [96]

---

[96] Luke 7:36-48

Teaching 67

Bless them that curse you and pray for
them that spitefully use you. [97]

---

[97] Matthew 5:44

Teaching 68

If your brother sins against you, go and tell him his fault, between you and him alone. If he listens to you, you have gained your brother.

But if he does not listen, take one or two others along with you, so that every word may be confirmed by the evidence of two or three witnesses.

If he refuses to listen to them, tell it to the church; and if he refuses to listen even to the church, let him be to you as a heathen and a tax collector.[98]

---

[98] Matthew 18:15-17

Teaching 69

Take heed to yourselves; if your brother sins, rebuke him, and if he repents, forgive him; and if he sins against you seven times in the day, and turns to you seven times, and says, "I repent," you must forgive him. [99]

Jesus says you should call people out for their misbehavior against you. Don't just keep it inside and hold a grudge against them. And because we all do wrong continually throughout our life, we must continually forgive.

---

[99] Luke 17:3-4

Teaching 70

The Parable of the Unforgiving Servant

Therefore, the Kingdom of Heaven is like a certain king, which would take account of his servants. And when he had begun to reckon, one was brought to him, which owed him ten thousand shekels.

But forasmuch as he had not to pay, his lord commanded him to be sold, and his wife, and children, and all that he had, and payment to be made.

The servant therefore fell down, and worshipped him, saying, Lord, have patience with me, and I will pay you all. Then the lord of that servant was moved

with compassion, and released him, and
forgave him the debt.

But the same servant went out, and found
one of his fellow servants, which owed him
a hundred pence: and he laid hands on him,
and took him by the throat, saying, Pay me
that which you owe.

And his fellow servant fell down at his feet,
and besought him, saying, "Have patience
with me, and I will pay you all." And he
would not: but went and cast him into
prison, till he should pay the debt.

So, when his fellow servants saw what was
done, they were very sorry, and came and
told their lord all that was done. Then his
lord, after that he had called him, said to

him, Oh you wicked servant, I forgave you all that debt, because you desired it of me:

Shouldest not you also have had compassion on your fellow servant, even as I had pity on you? And his lord was intensely angry, and delivered him to the tormentors, till he should pay all that was due to him.

So likewise, will my heavenly Father do also to you, if you from your hearts forgive not everyone his brother their trespasses. [100]

---

[100] Matthew 18:23-35

Teaching 71

For if you forgive people their mistakes, your heavenly Father will also forgive you:

But if you do not forgive people their mistakes, neither will your Father forgive your mistakes. [101]

---

[101] Matthew 6:14-15

Teaching 72

Then came Peter to him, and said, Lord, how often will my brother sin against me, and I forgive him? Up to seven times? Jesus said to him,

I don't tell you up to seven times, but, up to seventy times seven. [102]

---

[102] Matthew 18:21-22

Teaching 73

And when you stand praying, forgive, if you have anything against any: that your Father also which is in heaven may forgive you your trespasses.

But if you do not forgive, neither will your Father which is in heaven forgive your trespasses. [103]

Here Jesus says before you come to God with prayer, whether this is asking for forgiveness or as an act of religious devotion, it is more important to clear the slate with anyone you have some issue with, whether they have asked for forgiveness or not.

---

[103] Mark 11:25-26

Teaching 74

And forgive us our sins; for we also forgive everyone that is indebted to us. [104]

Teaching 75

And when they came to the place, which is called Calvary, there they crucified him, and the criminals, one on the right hand, and the other on the left. Then Jesus said,

Father, forgive them; for they know not what they do. [105]

---

[105] Luke 23:33-34

GOOD & EVIL, SIN & REPENTANCE

Jesus doesn't shy away from addressing the concepts of good and evil. He even states in one passage that there are wicked people placed on the earth by the adversary of humanity, Satan, to afflict the good people of the world.

This view of God being at war with the forces of darkness is a far cry from the near-universal view among believers and nonbelievers that God is so all-powerful that he must be allowing bad things to happen (or even creating them) and therefore bears responsibility for all suffering and evil. The real presence of profound evil in this world is rarely mentioned though we can see evidence of it every day.

A simplistic concept in which the evil of Satan and the malevolent people in the world bear no responsibility or power is often explained away by Christians as being for some mysterious good reason. Nonbelievers use the same flawed concept to argue against religion and the existence of a loving God who could permit evil and suffering. This ignores the numerous Bible passages conveying the struggle between good and evil and the strong power malevolence has in this world. Failing to acknowledge real evil and its power in this world and blaming everything on God makes humanity even more at risk of being evil's victim.

In the Christian Bible, a sin that controls you is equated with bondage and death. Jesus put an emphasis on rejecting old ways that limit life and on preaching right behavior among the people to help them live better lives and escape that bondage, rather than merely a means of placating an angry God. As with all true Christian principles, this is meant to serve you, not enslave you.

Repent from the Greek word metanoeō, means changing one's life by altering your conduct, attitude, and thinking, and returning to God's guidance for proper living, or simply to stop doing what you're doing wrong. This is a much softer and more sympathetic interpretation of what we often envision as demands for repentance as something thundering from the pulpit of an angry preacher.

Teaching 76

And it came to pass, as Jesus sat to eat in the house, behold, many publicans and sinners came and sat down with him and his disciples. And when the Pharisees saw it, they said to his disciples, Why does your master eat with publicans and sinners? But when Jesus heard that, he said to them,

The healthy do not need a physician, but those that are sick.

But go and learn what that means, I will have mercy, and not sacrifice: because I have not come to call the righteous, but sinners to repentance. [106]

---

[106] Matthew 9:12-13, Mark 2:17

Teaching 77

The Parable of the Weeds

Another parable Jesus put forward to them, saying,

The Kingdom of Heaven is like to a man
which sowed good seed in his field: But
while men slept, his enemy came and sowed
weeds among the wheat, and went his way.
But when the blade sprung up, and
brought forth fruit, then appeared the
weeds also.

So, the servants of the householder came
and said to him, "Sir, did you not plant
good seed in your field? From whence then
has it weeds?" He said to them, "An
enemy has done this." The servants said

to him, "Will you then that we go and gather them up?" But he said, "No; unless while you gather up the weeds, you root up also the wheat with them."

"Let both grow together until the harvest: and in the time of harvest, I will say to the reapers, Gather you together first the weeds, and bind them in bundles to burn them: but gather the wheat into my barns."

Then Jesus sent the multitude away and went into the house: and his disciples came to him, saying, "Declare to us the tares of the field." He answered and said to them,

He that sows the good seed is the Son of Man. The field is the world; the good seed are the children of the kingdom; but the weeds are the children of the wicked one; The enemy that sowed them is Satan; the harvest is the end of the world; and the reapers are the angels.

As therefore the tares are gathered and burned in the fire; so will it be in the end of this world. The Son of Man will send forth his angels, and they will gather out of his kingdom all things that offend, and them which do iniquity; And will cast them into a furnace of fire: there will be wailing and gnashing of teeth. Then will the righteous shine forth as the sun in the kingdom of their Father. Whoever has ears to hear, let him hear. [107]

---

[107] Matthew 13:3-30, Matthew 13:36-43

Teaching 78

Or what woman, if she had ten drachma coins, if she lost one drachma coin, wouldn't light a lamp, sweep the house, and seek diligently until she found it?

When she found it, she calls together her friends and neighbors, saying, "Celebrate with me, for I have found the drachma which I had lost."

Even so, I tell you, there is joy in the presence of the angels of God over one sinner repenting. [108]

Jesus is talking directly to us here. He's looking for sinners to join him, not the "already righteous." The

---

[108] Luke 15:8-10 (A drachma was worth about two days wages in first century Palestine.)

lesson is that a loving God rejoices when people see the error of their behavior and return to his ways, not that he is an angry and vengeful God anxiously waiting for an opportunity to punish and send people to hell for their mistakes.

Teaching 79

There were also others, two criminals, led with Jesus to be put to death. When they came to the place that is called "The Skull," they crucified him there with the criminals, one on the right and the other on the left.

Jesus said,

Father, forgive them, for they don't know what they are doing.

Dividing his garments among them, they rolled dice for them. The people stood watching.

The rulers with them also scoffed at him, saying, "He saved others. Let him save himself, if this is the Christ of God, his chosen one!"

The soldiers also mocked him, coming to him and offering him vinegar, and saying, "If you are the King of the Jews, save yourself!"

An inscription was also written over him in letters of Greek, Latin, and Hebrew: "THIS IS THE KING OF THE JEWS."

One of the criminals who was crucified insulted him, saying, "If you are the Christ, save yourself and us!"

But the other answered, and rebuking him said, "Don't you even fear God, seeing you are under the same condemnation?

And we indeed justly, for we receive the due reward for our deeds, but this man has done nothing wrong."

He said to Jesus, "Lord, remember me when you come into your Kingdom." Jesus said to him,

Assuredly I tell you, today you will be with me in Paradise. [109]

This scene at the crucifixion of Jesus shows that you can forgive people even if they don't ask for it, which most of us would naturally prefer. This passage does not advocate for waiting until the last possible minute to turn your life around, but it does show that this man crucified alongside Jesus didn't need an eight-step "Roman Road to Salvation." He knew he was getting a punishment that could be expected for his crimes, and he simply showed remorse and a belief that Jesus was who he claimed to be.

---

[109] Luke 23:32-43

Teaching 80

And if your hand causes you to sin, cut it off; it is better for you to enter life maimed than with two hands to go to hell, to the unquenchable fire.

And if your foot causes you to sin, cut it off; it is better for you to enter life lame than with two feet to be thrown into hell.

And if your eye causes you to sin, pluck it out; it is better for you to enter the Kingdom of God with one eye than with two eyes to be thrown into hell, where their ember does not die, and the fire is not quenched. [110]

---

[110] Matthew 5:29, Mark 9:43-48

Teaching 81

Now, early in the morning Jesus came again into the temple, and all the people came to him; and He sat down and taught them.

Then the scribes and Pharisees brought to him a woman caught in adultery. And when they had set her in the midst, they said to him, "Teacher, this woman was caught in adultery, in the very act. Now Moses, in the law, commanded us that such should be stoned. But what do You say?"

This they said, testing him, that they might have something of which to accuse him. But Jesus stooped down and wrote on the ground with his finger, as though He did not hear. So, when they continued asking him, He raised Himself up and said to them,

He who is without sin among you, let him throw a stone at her first.

And again, He stooped down and wrote on the ground. Then those who heard it, being convicted by their conscience, went out one by one, beginning with the oldest even to the last.

And Jesus was left alone, and the woman standing in the midst. When Jesus had raised Himself up and saw no one but the woman, He said to her,

Woman, where are those accusers of yours? Has no one condemned you?

She said, "No one, Lord." And Jesus said to her,

Neither do I condemn you; go and sin no more. [111]

---

[111] John 8:2-11

Teaching 82

You have heard that it was said by them of old time, "You will not commit adultery:"

But I say to you, That whoever looks at a woman to lust after her has committed adultery with her already in his heart. [112]

This simple yet powerful message goes beyond just a moral dimension to demonstrate the clear break from an outward, legalistic religious code to an inner, spiritual one.

---

[112] Matthew 5:27

THE GOOD NEWS

And it came to pass afterward, that he went throughout every city and village, preaching and showing the glad tidings of the kingdom of God: and the twelve were with him,

And certain women, which had been healed of evil spirits and infirmities, Mary called Magdalene, out of whom went seven devils, and Joanna the wife of Chuza Herod's steward, and Susanna, and many others, which ministered unto him of their possessions. [113]

You could fairly call all teachings of Jesus "The Good News" (translated from the Old English godspel), but I have tried to select the passages where he announces something particularly profound and foundational to the arrival of the Kingdom of God.

Jesus preached "glad tidings"—that clearly could not be perceived as "you're going to hell if you don't do what I say." The Good News was not a threat but a promise, not of a threat of eternal damnation, but a promise of peace, joy, enlightenment, forgiveness, love, generosity, fulfillment, and a new way of life. In a nutshell:

---

[113] Luke 8:1-3

- God loves you and is with you.
- You don't have to fear death.
- God wants you to be happy and peaceful.

You will often find that the Good News is that Jesus was crucified, died, and was resurrected based on their interpretation of verses such as Paul's first letter to the Corinthians verses 1-4.

An obvious practical question beyond the theological ones would be, "How could Jesus preach and tell his disciples to spread the message of his death and resurrection while he was still alive?" In addition, would anyone really hear that Jesus would be killed in the most horrific way imaginable and think that would be considered good news? Of course not.

While his death and resurrection are crucial in the mission of Jesus, and it is certainly good news that he suffered for us, risked death for speaking truth to power, and proved that death isn't the end of our existence, but it was not the core of his teachings to the masses or the message he told his disciples to spread after his death.

Of course, Jesus did not ignore the serious problems of sin and bad behavior against humanity and their consequences, but the Good News was a message of a new way of living that had been sent by God that brought hope, forgiveness, charity, love, and ethical living.

Embodied in these teachings are also the overarching themes that we don't need to fear death and that God loves us and wants us to be happy here on Earth.

Teaching 83

The Spirit of the Lord is upon me,
because he has anointed me to preach
good news to the poor.

He has sent me to proclaim release to the
captives and recovering of sight to the
blind, to set at liberty those who are
oppressed, to proclaim the acceptable
year of the Lord. [114]

---

[114] Luke 4:18-19

Teaching 84

Now after John was taken into custody, Jesus came into Galilee, preaching the Good News of God's Kingdom, and saying,

The time is fulfilled, and God's Kingdom is at hand! Repent, and believe in the Good News. [115]

---

[115] Matthew 4:12-13, 17, Mark 1:14-15

Teaching 85

For God so loved the world that He gave his only begotten Son, that whoever believes in him should not perish but have everlasting life.

For God did not send his Son into the world to condemn the world, but that the world through him might be saved. [116]

The first part of this passage is well known, particularly to anyone who watches NFL football broadcasts and has seen someone in the crowd holding up a John 3:16 poster. Lesser known, but equally important is verse 17 that follows.

---

[116] John 3:16-17

Teaching 86

I am come that they might have life, and
that they might have it more abundantly. [117]

---

[117] John 10:10

Teaching 87

Truly, truly, I say to you, if anyone keeps my word, he will never see death. [118]

---

[118] John 8:51

Teaching 88

I am the light of the world; he who follows me will not walk in darkness but will have the light of life. [119]

---

[119] John 8:12

Teaching 89

For the Son of Man is not come to destroy lives, but to save them. [120]

---

[120] Luke 9:56

Teaching 90

But love your enemies, and do good, and lend, expecting nothing in return; and your reward will be great, and you will be sons of the Most High; for he is kind to the ungrateful and the selfish.

Be merciful, even as your Father is merciful. [121]

---

[121] Matthew 5:43-48, Luke 6:27, Luke 6:34-36

Teaching 91

Come to me, all who labor and are heavily laden, and I will give you rest. Take my yoke upon you and learn from me; for I am gentle and lowly in heart, and you will find rest for your souls. For my yoke is easy, and my burden is light. [122]

---

[122] Matthew 11: 28-30

HEAVEN & HELL

I do not focus a lot of attention on Heaven and Hell in this book. That's because Jesus didn't either. What Jesus taught to the masses along the Sea of Galilee and in the hills of Judea he called Good News, not threats of eternal damnation.

Although the entertainment value of pondering the afterlife is no doubt irresistible, Jesus intimated that humans, even those fervently dedicated to religious study, barely understand earthly things so they should not obsess about the afterlife. We are to live simply, honestly, and with hope and optimism, as a child does, trusting in God and doing what is right.

Although there is the misconception that the Christian Bible focuses a great deal on Hell with the type of torments depicted in a Hieronymus Bosch painting, Jesus only spoke of Hell a few times, and those instances were overwhelmingly directed at the corrupt religious leaders of his day. Mistreatment of others and offending yourself through intentional sinful acts, not merely existing, exposes you to the danger of judgment.

The term for a place of punishment, Gehenna, in the Gospels appears different from the term Sheol or Hades, the home of the dead, or grave. The King James and most other English translations of the Bible use the word hell for both. It is believed that perhaps these represent the different schools of thought about the afterlife and belief in resurrection during Jesus' time.

A careful reading of Jesus' words suggests Hell exists for eternity, but that doesn't necessarily mean people will be there for eternity. He mentions scribes and Pharisees not being able to escape punishment or able to be released from punishment until their debt is paid.

Jesus also references some being punished more severely than others, e.g., "few stripes" versus "many stripes." The Gospels also mention people who will rise from the grave upon hearing Jesus' voice. There also seem to be at least two forms of Hell or at least two descriptions of it. One is a place of fiery torment, and the other is "outer darkness," a place of loneliness and separation from God.

Believe what you will about Near-Death Experiences (NDEs) and their scientific validity but there are rare accounts (most are a positive experience of peace and unconditional love) where people variously experienced both a place of intense spiritual suffering inhabited by demonic entities or a place of extreme loneliness and isolation from God's love and light.

If you are interested in the current scientific research into these afterlife phenomena, I suggest exploring the fascinating work on NDEs being done at the University of Virginia's Division of Perceptual Studies. (https://med.virginia.edu/perceptual-studies/)

Teaching 92

Let not your heart be troubled: ye believe in God, believe also in me.

In my Father's house are many mansions: if it were not so, I would have told you. I will go to prepare a place for you.

And if I go and prepare a place for you, I will come again, and receive you unto myself; that where I am, there ye may be also. [123]

---

[123] John 14:1-3

Teaching 93

Truly, truly, I say to you, We speak that which we know, and testify of that we have seen; and you did not accept our testimony.

If I have told you earthly things and you did not believe, how will you believe if I tell you of heavenly things? [124]

---

[124] John 3:11-12

Teaching 94

And that servant, who knew his lord's will, and prepared not himself, neither did according to his will, will be beaten with many stripes.

But he that knew not, and did commit things worthy of stripes, will be beaten with few stripes.

For to whomsoever much is given, of him will be much required: and to whom men have committed much, of him they will ask the more. [125]

---

[125] Luke 12:47-48

Teaching 95

Don't be afraid of those who kill the body but are not able to kill the soul. Rather, fear him who is able to destroy both soul and body in Hell. [126]

---

[126] Matthew 10:28, Luke 12:5

Teaching 96

And thou, Capernaum, which art exalted unto heaven, shalt be brought down to hell: for if the mighty works, which have been done in thee, had been done in Sodom, it would have remained until this day. [127]

---

[127] Matthew 11:23, Luke 10:15

Teaching 97

Truly I say to you, You will by no means come out thence, till you hast paid the uttermost penny. You serpents, you offspring of vipers, how will you escape the judgment of Gehenna? [128]

---

[128] Matthew 23:33

Teaching 98

If your right eye causes you to stumble, pluck it out and throw it away from you. For it is more profitable for you that one of your members should perish than for your whole body to be cast into Gehenna.

If your right hand causes you to stumble, cut it off, and throw it away from you. For it is more profitable for you that one of your members should perish, than for your whole body to be cast into Gehenna.

If your foot causes you to stumble, cut it off. It is better for you to enter into life lame, rather than having your two feet to be cast into Gehenna, into the fire that will never be quenched. [129]

Jesus is using extreme imagery here to make a point. He is not literally telling you to pluck your eye out. If you have a proclivity for a certain sin, e.g., envy, stealing, etc. this one character flaw could destroy your entire life if you don't stop doing it.

Most of us give ourselves a pass for having a single common weakness or two (overeating, laziness, excessive drinking, gambling, uncontrolled anger, jealousy, etc.), not realizing that even one of these is like a cancer that could destroy, not only our life but our soul.

---

[129] Matthew 5:29-30, Matthew 18:9, Mark 9:43-47

THE HOLY SPIRIT

Yes, you could spend a lifetime studying scriptures, analyzing all the arguments and current scholarship on every syllable as thousands have done over the centuries. That would not be time wasted if that is what you are called to do. But Jesus made it much simpler. The Holy Spirit would guide anyone who trusted him and listened to his words.

That is the purpose of this book. To present those words to you in their most simple original form, have you read them for yourself, and let the Holy Spirit reveal to you personally what no human can teach.

From my personal experience, I can attest this truly works. In times of struggle, I will instantly be reminded of the words of Jesus pertinent to my problem. Additionally, spiritual insight does not happen all at once, at least for me, it has taken a lifetime, ongoing and one day at a time. Nearly every time I read the Gospels, something new is revealed to me.

Teaching 99

But the Helper, the Holy Spirit, whom the Father will send in my name, He will teach you all things, and bring to your remembrance all things that I said to you. [130]

Here Jesus promises that the Spirit which God will send is the ultimate source of his spiritual knowledge and guidance, not books, philosophers, theologians, or clergy.

---

[130] John 14:26

Teaching 100

If you then, being evil, know how to give good gifts to your children, how much more will your heavenly Father give the Holy Spirit to those who ask him? [131]

---

[131] Luke 11:13

HOMOSEXUALITY

There are many Christian writers, preachers, and thought leaders whom I greatly admire and feel get everything right in interpreting the Gospels, except when it comes to the question of homosexuality. They flatly equate just being gay as a sin, despite how they might try to phrase their judgment. They often mistakenly associate being homosexual with all manner of promiscuity, debauchery, vulgarity, pornography, anti-Christian political agendas, immorality, or displays of kinky sexual fetishes at gay pride parades. Clearly, Jesus wouldn't condone any of these behaviors either in the gay or in the heterosexual community.

Invariably anti-gay religious individuals appeal to the Old Testament laws that they otherwise ignore. This is puzzling since a founding principle of Christianity is that if you appeal to the law of Moses you have to obey all of those laws.

They most often quote the book of Leviticus which waits until the 18th chapter and 22nd verse to state "Thou shalt not lie with mankind, as with womankind: it is abomination." They fail to mention that Leviticus also prescribes stoning for people picking up sticks on Saturdays and separating women from the community during menstruation. Leviticus also includes among the things that are an abomination eating: rabbits, any type of shellfish, swans, and certain, but not all, insects.

Strangely, the admonitions in Leviticus against defrauding your neighbor, charging interest on loans, fraudulently withholding wages from employees, mistreating the disabled, treating the rich with more deference than the poor, seeking revenge, not eating produce until the fifth year a tree has borne fruit, and getting tattoos or pierced ears are never mentioned by religious leaders.

What many Christians who condemn homosexuals as a group neglect to address is that Leviticus doesn't condemn women lying with women as with a man. Is lesbianism acceptable then? The passage is unexpectedly vague and brief in comparison to the level of detail for the other rules of dealing with menstruation, skin disorders, baldness, diet, preparation of meat, and ritual washing.

Oddly, it offers no prescribed punishments as it does for apparently much less serious offenses. Is what is being condemned the practice common in the classical world of men having sex with women strictly for procreation and saving sex with men and boys for pleasure? These "Old Testament Christians" also ignore that in a vision the Apostle Peter was told by Jesus that nothing God cleansed is to be considered unclean, in effect nullifying the dietary proclamations of Leviticus, and by extension the "unclean" concept.

Are we also obliged to carry out the death sentence for adultery? Or must we accept that the following people are blemished and not allowed to be priests: "a blind man, or a lame, or he that hath a flat nose, or anything superfluous, or a man that is broken footed, or broken handed, Or crookbacked, or a dwarf, or that hath a blemish in his eye, or be scurvy, or scabbed, or hath his stones (testicles) broken"? [132]

By not strictly obeying all the laws, Jesus says that you are a hypocrite if you proudly obey just the ones you like—or worse yet, use the laws to judge others and not yourself. Jesus reminds the Pharisees that whoever is guilty of part of the law is guilty of the entirety of the law if they live solely by it and not the greater law of God—mercy, justice, and forgiveness.

Consider also the relatively tepid reaction to the rampant sexual abuse of children by religious leaders in every faith community worldwide with the hysteria they exhibit about gay marriage. Compare the religious community's response with the dire warnings of Christ to those who abuse children. For those who still insist on appealing to the Old Testament or seemingly anti-homosexual statements in the post-Gospel New Testament, look at the rarely noted discussion of eunuchs in the book of Isaiah (56: 3-5):

Neither let the son of the foreigner, that has joined himself to the Lord, speak, saying, "The Lord has utterly separated me from his people; neither let the eunuch say, Behold, I am a dry tree."

---

[132] Leviticus 21:18-21

For thus says the Lord to the eunuchs that keep my Sabbaths, and choose the things that please me, and take hold of my covenant: Even to them will I give in mine house and within my walls a place and a name better than of sons and of daughters; I will give them an everlasting name, that will not be cut off.

In the near-universal belief on both sides of the debate that Jesus never said anything about same-sex relationships, many explanations typically take the form of something like, "It was so obvious that Jesus was against it because the law of Moses is so clear there was no need for him to say anything."

Despite the vast number of Christian thinkers who say Jesus never mentions homosexuality, the following is a single cryptic passage from the book of Matthew that appears to address the issue. This is a teaching that seems to have been largely overlooked and ignored for centuries.

Teaching 101

All men cannot receive this saying, except they to whom it is given.

For there are some eunuchs, who were so born from their mother's womb; and there are some eunuchs, who were made eunuchs by men; and there are eunuchs, who have made themselves eunuchs for the Kingdom of Heaven's sake. [133]

The passage above appears in the first book of the New Testament and takes place immediately after Jesus' famous admonition against frivolous divorce. How he mentions the hardness of people's hearts being the reason for these laws is significant.

Just as Jesus avoided death several times by carefully choosing his words and speaking enigmatically on volatile topics (for example, not repeatedly shouting, "I am the Son of God!" in the

---

synagogue before people who would have stoned him immediately), it seems probable that he offered his insights in a way that would have been revealed to those who took time to carefully consider his words. "Whoever has ears to hear, let him hear," he often said.

He speaks of people as being eunuchs because that is their natural state ("born that way," people who are eunuchs because they have been made that way by men (through childhood trauma and/or sexual abuse). If we are to see Jesus in the context of having Godly insight or profound enlightenment, it is easy to see that he would recognize that some people are born sexually different, some then, as now, have their sexuality altered by sexual abuse as children or other profound psychological influences. The third broad group he mentions enigmatically are those who are "made eunuchs for the Kingdom of Heaven's sake." What does that mean? Only those to whom God chooses to reveal it?

If one were to try to argue this is specifically referring only to physical castration, Jesus' championing of outcasts once again comes around to make the exclusion of anyone who would follow him indefensible. As noted in Deuteronomy 23:1, anyone "wounded in the stones or having his private member cut off," will not enter into the congregation of the Lord. If these people are forbidden by Hebrew law to join the congregation, why then does Jesus say they can be eunuchs for the Kingdom of Heaven's sake?

Perhaps the era where women, Gentiles, the disabled, and society's outcasts were not allowed in the most exclusive parts of God's Temple had come to an end.

Furthermore, there were no dictates of celibacy in the church for more than 1,000 years after this statement was made and castration certainly wasn't practiced among Judeans and would not become commonplace in the Levant for centuries to come.

So, how could he have been referring only to castrated men? Could this be a cryptic reference to the Essenes, many of whom practiced celibacy and, like Jesus, and John the Baptist, used ritual immersion in water as a metaphor for spiritual purification, or simply a prediction of the role homosexuals would play in Christianity?

THE KINGDOM OF GOD /
THE KINGDOM OF HEAVEN

Whether the term Kingdom of Heaven is synonymous with Kingdom of God has been vigorously debated as has virtually every word of the Gospels, but it seems most likely they are interchangeable, as evidenced by Matthew using both terms in close proximity. Only Matthew uses the expression Kingdom of Heaven in the parallel passages and in the same context as Mark and Luke, providing further evidence that it was synonymous with the Kingdom of God.

Heaven and *God* perhaps were used in different contexts to avoid confusion with a Gentile audience who might have known heaven as the adobe of pagan gods. However, there is evidence, though subtle, in the following verses that the phrase meant several things. Some seem to hint at the stewardship of God's domain on earth by the Israelites before the arrival of John and Jesus, at which time a new or more perfect Kingdom was coming into being and would be completed upon the death and resurrection of Jesus.

That may be too theological for our purposes here, so read on and see what you think. The bottom line is that the Kingdom is not an earthly religious edifice but an inner spiritual one.

Teaching 102

Because it is given to you to know the mysteries of the Kingdom of Heaven, but to them it is not given.

For whoever has, to him will be given, and he will have more abundance: but whoever has not, from him will be taken away even that he has.

Therefore, speak I to them in parables: because seeing they see not; and hearing they hear not, neither do they understand. [134]

---

[134] Mathew 13:11-13

Teaching 103

Now when He was asked by the Pharisees when the Kingdom of God would come, He answered them and said,

The Kingdom of God does not come with observation; nor will they say, "See here!" or "See there!" For indeed, the Kingdom of God is within you. [135]

---

[135] Luke 17:20-21

Teaching 104

And they brought young children to him, that he should bless them; and his disciples rebuked those who brought them. But when Jesus saw it, he was very displeased and said to them,

Allow the little children to come to me, and forbid them not, for of such is the Kingdom of God.

Truly I say to you, whoever will not receive the Kingdom of God as a little child, he will not enter there.

And he took them up in his arms, put his hands upon them, and blessed them. [136]

---

[136] Matthew 19:14, Mark 10:14-15, Luke 18:16

There are many layers of meaning to this passage, but one of them is that you cannot receive the Kingdom with your intellect. It requires deeper understanding on a purely spiritual level with the trust, openness, and optimism of a child.

Teaching 105

You are the salt of the earth: but if the salt has lost its savor, wherewith will it be salted? it is thenceforth good for nothing, but to be cast out, and to be trodden under foot of men.

You are the light of the world. A city that is set on a hill cannot be hidden.

Neither do men light a candle, and put it under a bushel, but on a candlestick; and it giveth light to all that are in the house.

Let your light so shine before men, that they may see your good works, and glorify your Father which is in heaven.

Think not that I am come to destroy the
law, or the prophets: I am not come to
destroy, but to fulfill.

For Truly I say to you, Till heaven and
earth pass, one jot or one tittle will in no
way pass from the law, until all be fulfilled.

Whoever therefore will break one of these
least commandments, and will teach men so,
he will be called the least in the Kingdom
of Heaven: but whoever will do and teach
them, the same will be called great in the
Kingdom of Heaven. [137]

---

[137] Matthew 5:13-19

Teaching 106

Truly, I say to you, unless you turn and become like children, you will never enter the Kingdom of Heaven.

Whoever humbles himself like this child, he is the greatest in the Kingdom of Heaven.

Whoever receives one such child in my name receives me; but whoever causes one of these little ones who believe in me to sin, it would be better for him to have a great millstone fastened round his neck and to be drowned in the depth of the sea. [138]

---

[138] Matthew 18:3-6

Teaching 107

The Kingdom of Heaven is like a grain of mustard seed which a man took, and sowed in his field, which indeed is smaller than all seeds.

But when it is grown, it is greater than the herbs and becomes a tree, so that the birds of the air come and lodge in its branches. [139]

There are many interpretations of this passage including that it was a prediction that the tiny Jesus movement would grow and spread to all people of the world. It could also be fairly interpreted to mean that the Kingdom of Heaven, once introduced into a person's life, will expand into the most important aspect of their existence.

---

[139] Matthew 13:31-32, Mark 4:31, Luke 13:19

Teaching 108

And from the days of John the Baptist until now the Kingdom of Heaven is controlled by force, and the powerful took it by force.

For all the prophets and the law prophesied until John. And if you will receive it, this is Elias, who was to come.

He that has ears to hear, let him hear. [140]

The KJV translates force and powerful as violence and violent, respectively. I've used the Aramaic translation for those words to convey that, like governments, the Israelite religion had been controlled by dominant men in a legalistic and authoritarian way with hopes of a violent overthrow of their oppressors and the arrival of the Messiah. Now, the true Kingdom is here as an unseen state requiring spiritual power, not force.

---

[140] Matthew 11:12-15

Teaching 109

The blind receive their sight, and the lame walk, the lepers are cleansed, and the deaf hear, the dead are raised up, and the poor have the gospel preached to them. And blessed is he, whoever will not be offended in me.

And as they departed, Jesus began to say to the multitudes concerning John,

What did you go out into the wilderness to see? A reed shaken with the wind? But what did you go out to see? A man clothed in soft clothing? Behold, they that wear soft clothing are in kings' houses. But what did you go out to see? A prophet?

Yes, I say to you, and more than a prophet. For this is he, of whom it is written, "Behold, I send my messenger before your face, which will prepare your way before you."

Truly I say to you, Among them that are born of women there has not risen a greater than John the Baptist: notwithstanding he that is least in the Kingdom of Heaven is greater than he. [141]

Not meant to denigrate John the Baptist, this passage is often taken to mean that those who will come to know the full life and ministry of Jesus will have a greater understanding and experience of the true Kingdom that John was not able to see fulfilled before he was executed.

---

[141] Matthew 11:5-11

Teaching 110

As they went on the way, a certain man said to him, "I want to follow you wherever you go, Lord." Jesus said to him,

The foxes have holes, and the birds of the sky have nests, but the Son of Man has no place to lay his head.

He said to another,

Follow me!

But he said, "Lord, allow me first to go and bury my father." But Jesus said to him,

Leave the dead to bury their own dead, but you go and announce God's Kingdom. [142]

This admonition to "Leave the dead bury their own dead," sounds unbelievably harsh, but "allow me first to go and bury my father" is an ancient near east idiom meaning, "Let me wait until my father dies, i.e., I've gotten my inheritance first."

---

[142] Matthew 8:21-22, Luke 9:57-60

Teaching 111

The Parables of the Hidden Treasure, The Expensive Pearl & The Net

Again, the Kingdom of Heaven is like treasure hidden in a field, which when a man has found, he hides, and for joy thereof goes and sells all that he has and buys that field.

Again, the Kingdom of Heaven is like a merchant man, seeking large pearls: Who, when he had found one pearl of great price, went and sold all that he had, and bought it.

Again, the Kingdom of Heaven is like a net, that was cast into the sea, and gathered of every kind: Which, when it was full, they drew to shore, and sat down, and gathered the good into vessels, but cast the bad away.

So will it be at the end of the world: the angels will come forth, and sever the wicked from among the just, And will cast them into the furnace of fire: there will be wailing and gnashing of teeth. [143]

The challenge is to find the truth amid all the confusion, disinformation, and distortion. You cannot let the failings of church leaders or Christians, or your negative experiences with religion keep you from the great spiritual truths and gifts of God.

---

[143] Matthew 13:44-50

THE NATURE OF GOD

"God" is mentioned more than 270 times in The Gospels and the term "Father" is used in reference to him more than 250 times. In most passages Jesus refers to the things God does, how he works, and what he wants, but very little about his nature and offers no in-depth theological exploration of who God is.

This is consistent with how Jesus portrayed his disciples' inability at times to understand even simple spiritual concepts. Indeed, most of us could not pass a college-level organic chemistry course, so how could we possibly understand the creator of the universe?

However, it is clear that God, as a spirit, does not have a human physical qualities, race, or preference for a single ethnic group. Neither can God be narrowly defined or served by only one religious doctrine, dogma, or liturgy.

Teaching 112

God is spirit, and those who worship him must worship him in spirit and in truth. [144]

There you have it. The sum total of what Jesus said directly about the nature of God. So clearly as spirit, God is neither male nor female. Those are earthly physical attributes. The fact that Jesus doesn't go into great detail about the nature of God is telling.

God is unknowable to human understanding beyond what Jesus reveals about his qualities of kindness, generosity, and love, or what God reveals to his children through the Holy Spirit. We are to focus on doing God's will. His presence within us and in the natural world around us should be self-evident.

---

[144] John 4:24

PEACE & LOVE

It is important to remember how important this message of Jesus is. Although this is widely viewed as the essence of the one-dimensional view of Jesus, it is often lost in the doctrines of Christian churches and in theology, which alternately seem to focus either on the crucifixion of Jesus or on sin or heaven and hell.

Any academic debates on the meaning or interpretation of scriptures must hang on Jesus' teachings on peace and love. A spiritual life focused on love and all its dimensions makes the vast majority of debates and theological arguments superfluous.

Teaching 113

Love God with all your heart, and with all your soul, and with all your mind.

This is the first and great commandment, and the second is like it, love your neighbor as yourself. [145]

---

[145] Matthew 22:37, Mark 12:30, Luke 10:27

Teaching 114

Have peace one with another. [146]

Teaching 115

As the Father loved me, I also have loved you; abide in my love. If you keep my commandments, you will abide in my love, just as I have kept my Father's commandments and abide in his love. [147]

---

[147] John 15:9-10

Teaching 116

A new commandment I give to you, that you love one another; even as I have loved you, that you also love one another.

By this all men will know that you are my disciples, if you have love for one another. [148]

---

[148] John 13:33-35

Teaching 117

This is my commandment, that you love one another as I have loved you. Greater love has no man than this, that a man lay down his life for his friends. [149]

---

[149] John 15:12-13

Teaching 118

You have heard that it was said, "An eye for an eye, and a tooth for a tooth."

But I tell you, don't resist him who is evil; but whoever strikes you on your right cheek, turn to him the other also. If anyone sues you to take away your coat, let him have your cloak also.

Teaching 119

And to him that strikes you on the one cheek, offer also the other; and him that takes away your shirt, forbid not to take your coat also.

But I say to you, That you resist not evil: but whoever will smite you on your right cheek, turn to him the other also.

And if any man will sue you at the law, and take away your coat, let him have your cloak also. [150]

---

[150] Matthhew 5:39-40, Luke 6:29

PRAYER

A 2018 Harvard Study by renowned mind-body researcher Dr. Howard Benson and his team showed that meditating for just 15 minutes per day may reduce blood pressure in patients with coronary heart disease, increase attention span, and cause alterations in the expression of 172 genes regulating glucose metabolism, circadian rhythms, and inflammation. Dr. Benson's research has also shown that prayer and related meditative practices have similar effects.

Other university studies have shown that those who prayed or meditated for one-half hour daily caused measurable changes in gray-matter density in parts of the brain linked with sense of self and empathy and that this increased brain tissue in the hippocampus, an area key to learning and memory, also indicated a decrease in anxiety and stress.

You may note that Jesus' guidance on public prayer doesn't promote such practices as prayer at football games and political rallies, or even in front of a church congregation, but prayer is something for God's ears, not to demonstrate your righteousness.

Teaching 120

But you, when you pray, enter your closet, and when you have shut your door, pray to your Father who is in secret; and your Father who sees in secret will reward you openly.

But when you pray, use not vain repetitions, as the pagans do: for they think that they will be heard for their much speaking.

Be not you therefore like to them: for your Father knows what things you have need of, before you ask him. [151]

---

[151] Matthew 6:6-8

Teaching 121

The Lord's Prayer

Pray like this: Our Father, who is in heaven, Sacred is your name. Your kingdom come. Your will be done, On earth as it is in heaven.

Give us this day our daily bread; And forgive us our debts, As we also have forgiven our debtors.

And let us not be led into temptation but deliver us from evil. [152]

Jesus doesn't say to pray this prayer exactly and repetitiously but, in this manner, and in this spirit.

---

[152] Matthew 6:9-13

Teaching 122

The Parable of the Persistent Widow

He also spoke a parable to them that they must always pray, and not give up, saying,

There was a judge in a certain city who didn't fear God and didn't respect man. A widow was in that city, and she often came to him, saying, "Defend me from my adversary!"

He wouldn't for a while, but afterward he said to himself, "Though I neither fear God, nor respect man, yet because this widow bothers me, I will defend her, or else she will wear me out by her continual coming."

The Lord said,

Listen to what the unrighteous judge says. Won't God avenge his chosen ones who are crying out to him day and night, and yet he exercises patience with them? I tell you that he will avenge them quickly.

Nevertheless, when the Son of Man comes, will he find faith on the earth?" [153]

---

[153] Luke 18:1-8

Teaching 123

Watch and pray that you don't enter into temptation. The spirit indeed is willing, but the flesh is weak. [154]

---

[154] Matthew 26:41, Mark 14:38

SALVATION &
BEING BORN AGAIN

One of the more stunning things to me as a Christian is the common Evangelical prescription for what it takes to be "saved," in the so-called Roman Road to Salvation. This is a collection of various verses taken from Paul's letters to the early Christian church in Rome, outlining the path to salvation.

Some versions include one verse from the Gospels, John 3:16. Most versions, however, completely ignore anything Jesus had to say about salvation and rely solely on the post-Gospel opinion of the disciple Paul. The Roman Road usually includes some or all of the following:

Romans 3:23
"...for all have sinned and fall short of the glory of God..."

Romans 5:1
"Therefore, since we have been justified through faith, we have peace with God through our Lord Jesus Christ."

Romans 5:8
"But God demonstrates his own love toward us, in that while we were still sinners, Christ died for us."

Romans 6:23

"For the wages of sin is death, but the gracious gift of God is eternal life in Christ Jesus our Lord."

Romans 8:1

"Therefore, there is now no condemnation for those who are in Christ..."

Romans 10:9

"...that if you confess with your mouth Jesus as Lord, and believe in your heart that God raised him from the dead, you will be saved..."

Romans 10:13

"for everyone who calls on the name of the Lord will be saved."

Not that anything in the verses above used in the Roman Road is objectionable or unhelpful, except that they don't include one word spoken by Jesus! Nor do they contain any of the subtlety of salvation spoken of by Jesus as both instantaneous and ongoing.

If you read the teachings contained in the Gospels, it becomes clear that what Jesus said about salvation was more of a holistic spiritual approach that encompasses changes in mind, body, and spirit, and requires a radical change in behavior versus a simple profession of faith.

Salvation as a concept also varied from one Gospel situation to the next. The thief crucified with Jesus merely asks Christ to remember him and is told he will be with him in Paradise. In another passage, Jesus says "Who endures to the end will be saved."

Salvation isn't a contract or a legal process like joining a club, but a comprehensive and continual inward revolution in your heart, mind, and soul that should radically alter your worldview as well as your actions.

Teaching 124

And behold, a certain lawyer stood up and tested him, saying, "Master, what will I do to inherit eternal life?" Jesus said to him,

What is written in the law? How do you read it?

And he answered saying, "You will love the Lord your God with all your heart, and with all your soul, and with all your strength, and with all your mind, and your neighbor as yourself." And Jesus said to him,

You have answered correctly; do this, and you will live.

But he, wanting to justify himself, said to Jesus, "And who is my neighbor?" And Jesus in answering said,

A certain man went down from Jerusalem to Jericho and fell among thieves, who stripped him of his clothes and wounded him, and left, leaving him half dead. And by chance, a certain priest came that way.

And when he saw him, he passed by on the other side. And likewise, a Levite, when he was at the place, came and looked on him and passed by on the other side.

But a certain Samaritan, as he journeyed, came to where he was. And when he saw him, he had compassion on him, and went to him and bound up his wounds, pouring on

oil and wine; and he set him on his own
beast, and brought him to an inn and took
care of him.
And on the next day when he departed, he
took out two pence, and gave them to the
host and said to him, "Take care of him;
and whatever more you spend, when I come
again, I will repay you."

Now which of these three, do you think,
was neighbor to him that fell among the
thieves?

And he said, "He that showed mercy on
him." Then said Jesus to him,

Go and do you likewise. [155]

---

[155] Luke 10:25-37

The Samaritans originated from the ancient Israelite tribes but emerged as a distinct group after the northern Kingdom of Israel was conquered by the Assyrians in 720 BC. Some Israelites migrated to the southern kingdom of Judah (the Judeans or Jews) while the Israelites that stayed in Samaria came to be known as Samaritans.

As the Samaritans emerged as a distinct ethno-religious community, the Judeans came to regard them as not pure Israelites, but a mix of Assyrians and other ethnic groups settled in the region after the conquest. The Jews held similar views about the Galileans.

Core tenets of the Samaritan faith are the belief that worship should be at Mount Gerizim instead of the Temple in Jerusalem and that the Samaritan Pentateuch is the authentic version of the Torah.

When the Maccabean king destroyed the Mount Gerizim temple and brought Samaria under his rule in the second century BC, it led to intense animosity between Jews and Samaritans so that by the time of Jesus, Second Temple Judaism and Samaritanism were largely considered separate religions.

Teaching 125

For the Son of Man is not come to destroy lives, but to save them. [156]

---

[156] Luke 9:56

Teaching 126

I am the door: by me, if any man enters in, he will be saved, and will go in and out, and find pasture.

The thief comes to steal, and to kill, and to destroy. I have come that they might have life and that they might have it more abundantly.

I am the good shepherd: the good shepherd gives his life for the sheep. But he that is a hired hand, and not the shepherd, whose own the sheep are not, sees the wolf coming, and leaves the sheep, and flees: and the wolf catches them, and scatters the sheep.

The hired hand flees, because he is a hired hand, and cares not for the sheep. I am the good shepherd, and know my sheep, and am known by mine. As the Father knows me, even so know I the Father: and I lay down my life for the sheep. [157]

Both Christians and Christianity's opponents point to the first sentence above either as proof that Heaven is for Christians only or, conversely, that Christianity is too unaccepting of other religions as a path to God.

Without delving into the validity of Near-Death Experiences there are many accounts of those who have NDEs meeting someone they perceived as Jesus at the entrance to the afterlife refusing to let them enter because their work on earth is unfinished.

This makes more sense in the totality of what Jesus said regarding, "No one comes to the Father but by me." Perhaps Jesus is simply saying that he is showing the correct path, and he will decide who enters the Kingdom in this life and in the hereafter, rather than,

---

[157] John 10:9

"You have to call yourself a follower of me or follow a particular church creed to be saved." He certainly didn't say that people on earth would get to decide who goes to heaven or hell

Teaching 127

For God so loved the world, that he gave his only begotten Son, that whosoever believeth in him should not perish, but have everlasting life.

For God sent not his Son into the world to condemn the world; but that the world through him might be saved. [158]

---

[158] John 3:16-17

Teaching 128

There was a man of the Pharisees, named Nicodemus, a ruler of the Jews: the same came to Jesus by night, and said to him, "Rabbi, we know that you are a teacher come from God: for no man can do these miracles that you do, except God be with him." Jesus answered and said to him,

Truly, Truly I say to you, Except a man be born again, he cannot see the Kingdom of God.

Nicodemus said to him, "How can a man be born when he is old? Can he enter the second time into his mother's womb, and be born?" Jesus answered,

Absolutely, I say to you, Except a man be born of water and of the Spirit, he cannot enter into the Kingdom of God. That which is born of the flesh is flesh; and that which is born of the Spirit is spirit.

Marvel not that I said to you, You must be born again. The wind blows where it wants, and you hear the sound of it, but cannot tell where it comes from or where it's going; so is everyone that is born of the Spirit. [159]

Note that Jesus says here, "Except a man be born again, he cannot see the Kingdom of God." This seems to portray being Born Again as a transformative way of seeing the Kingdom of God that can exist within you, rather than an assertion of theology, or a place to enter

---

[159] John 3:1-8

at some future date. In other words, it is already here if you have eyes to see it.

This new view of your world will in turn guide your actions. If you view life and humanity in a new light and with a new perspective, you don't need hundreds of strict rules and religious laws to guide your every action.

Teaching 129

For God so loved the world, that he gave his only begotten Son, that whosoever believes in him should not perish, but have everlasting life.

For God sent not his Son into the world to condemn the world; but that the world through him might be saved.

He that believes on him is not condemned: but he that believes not is condemned already, because he has not believed in the name of the only begotten Son of God.

And this is the condemnation, that light is come into the world, and men loved

darkness rather than light, because their
deeds were evil.

For everyone that does evil hates the light,
neither comes to the light, unless his deeds
should be criticized.

But he that does truth comes to the light,
that his deeds may be made evident, that
they are wrought in God. [160]

---

[160] John 3:16-21

Teaching 130

For the Son of Man is come to save that which was lost. What do you think? If a man has a hundred sheep, and one of them be gone astray, does he not leave the ninety and nine, and go into the mountains, and seek that which is gone astray?

And if so be that he find it, Truly I say to you, he rejoices more for that sheep than for the ninety-nine which did not go astray. Even so, it is not the will of your Father which is in heaven that one of these little ones should perish. [161]

---

[161] Matthew 18:11-14

Teaching 131

The Parable of the Prodigal Son

And he said, A certain man had two sons: And the younger of them said to his father, Father, give me the portion of goods that falls to me. And he divided to them his living.

And not many days after the younger son gathered all together, and took his journey into a far country, and there wasted his substance with riotous living.

And when he had spent all, there arose a mighty famine in that land; and he began to be in want.

And he went and joined himself to a citizen
of that country, and he sent him into his
fields to feed swine.

And he would have been willing to have
filled his belly with the husks that the swine
ate and no man gave to him.

And when he came to himself, he said,
How many hired servants of my father
have bread enough and to spare, and I
perish with hunger! I will arise and go to my
father and will say to him, Father, I have
sinned against heaven, and before you.

And I am no longer worthy to be called
your son: make me one of your hired
servants.

And he arose and came to his father. But when he was still a great way off, his father saw him, and had compassion, and ran, and fell on his neck, and kissed him. And the son said to him, Father, I have sinned against heaven, and in your sight, and am no more worthy to be called your son.

But the father said to his servants, Bring forth the best robe, and put it on him; and put a ring on his hand, and shoes on his feet: And bring hither the fatted calf, and kill it; and let us eat, and be merry: For this my son was dead, and is alive again; he was lost, and is found. And they began to be merry.

Now his elder son was in the field: and as he came and drew near to the house, he heard music and dancing.

And he called one of the servants and asked what these things meant. And he said to him, Your brother is come; and your father has killed the fatted calf, because he has received him safe and sound.

And he was angry, and would not go in, so his father came out and pleaded with him.

And he said to his father, these many years do I serve you, neither transgressed I at any time your commandment: and yet you never gave me a goat, that I might make merry with my friends: But as soon as your other son arrives, who has devoured your fortune with prostitutes, you have killed for him the fatted calf.

And he said to him, Son, you are always with me, and all that I have is yours. It was appropriate that we should make merry and be glad: for this your brother was dead, and is alive again; and was lost, and is found. [162]

---

[162] Luke 15:11-32

Teaching 132

At the same time came the disciples to Jesus, saying, Who is the greatest in the Kingdom of Heaven?

And Jesus called a little child to him and set him in the midst of them and said,

Truly I say to you, except you be changed, and become as little children, you will not enter the Kingdom of Heaven.

Whosoever therefore will humble himself as this little child, the same is greatest in the Kingdom of Heaven.

And whoso will receive one such little child in my name receives me.

But whoever will offend one of these little ones which believe in me, it were better for him that a millstone were hanged about his neck, and that he were drowned in the depth of the sea.

Woe to the world because of offenses! For it must be that offenses come; but woe to that man by whom the offense comes! [163]

---

[163] Matthew 18:1-7

Teaching 133

Jesus, knowing that the Father had given all things into his hands, and that he came from God, and was going to God, arose from supper, and laid aside his outer garments.

He took a towel and wrapped a towel around his waist. Then he poured water into the basin and began to wash the disciples' feet and to wipe them with the towel that was wrapped around him. Then he came to Simon Peter. He said to him, "Lord, do you wash my feet?"

Jesus answered him,

You don't know what I am doing now, but you will understand later.

Peter said to him, "You will never wash my feet!" Jesus answered him,

If I don't wash you, you have no part with me.

Simon Peter said to him, "Lord, not my feet only, but also my hands and my head!" Jesus said to him,

Someone who has bathed only needs to have his feet washed but is completely clean. You are clean, but not all of you.

For he knew who would betray him, therefore he said,

You are not all clean.

So, when he had washed their feet, put his outer garment back on, and sat down again, he said to them,

Do you know what I have done to you? You call me, "Teacher" and "Lord." You say so correctly, for so I am. If I then, the Lord and the Teacher, have washed your feet, you also ought to wash one another's feet. For I have given you an example, that you should also do as I have done to you. [164]

These passages are typically portrayed as an exercise in humility and service, but there seems to be something deeper going on here. After visiting a Roman bath or a ritual Jewish bath in ancient times in which the whole body would be cleansed, the feet would become dirty again after walking home in sandals and would need to be washed again.

---

[161] John 13:3-15

Jesus seems to be making a parallel to the disciples (and all children of God) that they have been washed and made clean by God, but he cleanses them from the daily transgressions they accumulate as they walk through this world. He charges them to do likewise, offering future disciples that service to help cleanse others through following his example and spreading his message.

Teaching 134

Truly, Truly I tell you, he who hears my word and believes him who sent me has eternal life, and doesn't come into judgment, but has passed out of death into life.

Truly, Truly I tell you, the hour is coming, and now is, when the dead will hear the Son of God's voice; and those who hear will live. [165]

Jesus makes it clear that all that is needed to avoid spiritual death is to hear his words and believe in the God who sent him. In keeping with the mystical nature of John's Gospel, Jesus goes on to say in verses 26-29 that those in the grave will hear his voice and come out to be judged by their deeds.

---

[165] John 5:24-25

Teaching 135

He went on his way through cities and villages, teaching, and traveling on to Jerusalem. One said to him, "Lord, are they few who are saved?" He said to them,

Strive to enter by the narrow door; for many, I tell you, will seek to enter and will not be able.

When the master of the house has risen up, and has shut the door, and you begin to stand outside and to knock at the door, saying, "Lord, Lord, open to us!" then he will answer and tell you, "I don't know you or where you come from." [166]

---

[166] Luke 13:22-24

Salvation and entering the Kingdom requires sincere effort and cannot be faked or taken with shortcuts.

SPIRITUALITY & SEEKING GOD

The last words of former Beatle George Harrison before he succumbed to cancer were reported to be, "Everything else can wait, but the search for God cannot wait, and love one another." This profound sentiment epitomizes recognition of the importance of a spiritual life and echoes the core themes of Jesus' teachings in their directness and simplicity.

Christian spirituality cannot be understood as an academic discipline or intellectual enterprise. True religion is not a cult, but a necessary part of life as essential to happiness as art, music, friendship, good food, and health.

It should be noted that Jesus used prayer and fasting as key components of his spiritual life to achieve altered state of consciousness and healing, not hallucinogenic drugs.

Teaching 136

But the hour is coming, and now is when the true worshipers will worship the Father in spirit and truth, for such the Father seeks to worship him. [167]

---

[167] John 4:23

Teaching 137

At that time Jesus answered and said,

I thank you, Father, Lord of heaven and earth, because you have hidden these things from the wise and prudent and have revealed them to children. [168]

---

[168] Matthew 11:25-27

Teaching 138

All things are delivered to me of my
Father: and no man knows the Son, but
the Father; neither knows any man the
Father, save the Son and they to whom
the Son will reveal him. [169]

---

[169] Matthew 11:27

Teaching 139

Ask, and it will be given to you. Seek, and you will find.

Knock, and it will be opened for you. For everyone who asks receives. He who seeks finds. To him who knocks it will be opened.

Or who is there among you who, if his son asks him for bread, will give him a stone? Or if he asks for a fish, who will give him a serpent?

If you then, being evil, know how to give good gifts to your children, how much more will your Father who is in heaven give good things to those who ask him? [170]

---

[170] Matthew 7:7-11, Luke 11:9-13

Teaching 140

The Parable of the Sower

Behold, a farmer went forth to sow; And when he sowed, some seeds fell by the wayside, and the fowls came and devoured them up: Some fell upon stony places, where they had not much earth: and forthwith they sprung up, because they had no deepness of earth: And when the sun was up, they were scorched; and because they had no root, they withered away.

And some fell among thorns; and the thorns sprung up and choked them: But others fell into good ground, and brought forth fruit, some a hundred times, some

sixty times, some thirty times. Who has
ears to hear, let him hear.

And the disciples came, and said to him,
Why speak you to them in parables? he
answered and said to them,

Because it is given to you to know the
mysteries of the Kingdom of Heaven, but
to them it is not given. For whoever has, to
him will be given, and he will have more
abundance: but whoever has not, from him
will be taken away even that he has.

Therefore, speak I to them in parables:
because they seeing see not; and hearing
they hear not, neither do they understand.

And in them is fulfilled the prophecy of Isaiah, which said, "By hearing you will hear, and will not understand; and seeing you will see, and will not perceive:

For this people's heart is waxed gross, and their ears are dull of hearing, and their eyes they have closed; lest at any time they should see with their eyes, and hear with their ears, and should understand with their heart, and should be converted, and I should heal them."

But blessed are your eyes, for they see and your ears, for they hear. For Truly I say to you, That many prophets and righteous men have desired to see those things which you see and have not seen

them; and to hear those things which you
hear and have not heard them.

Hear you therefore the Sower.
When anyone hears the word of the
kingdom, and understands it not, then
comes from the wicked one, and catches
away that which was sown in his heart.

This is he which received seed by the
wayside. But he that received the seed into
stony places, the same is he that hears the
word, and immediately with joy receives it.

Yet has no root in himself but endures for
a while: for when tribulation or persecution
arises because of the word, by and by he is
offended. He also that received seed
among the thorns is he that hears the word;

254

and the cares of this world, and the deceitfulness of riches, choke the word, and he becomes unfruitful.

But he that received seed into the good ground is he that hears the word, and understands it, which also bears fruit, and brings forth, some a hundredfold, some sixty, some thirty. [171]

---

[171] Matthew 13:3-23, Mark 4:3-20, Luke 8:5-18

Teaching 141

Don't work for the food which perishes, but for the food which remains to eternal life, which the Son of Man will give to you. For God the Father has sealed him. [172]

---

[172] John 6:27

Teaching 142

Whoever drinks of the water that I will give will never thirst again; but the water that I will give them will become a well of water springing up to eternal life. [173]

---

[173] John 4:14

Teaching 143

The Parable of the Banquet

A man gave a great dinner to which he invited many. When the time for the dinner came, he dispatched his servant to say to those invited, "Come, everything is now ready."

But one by one, they all began to excuse themselves. The first said to him, "I have purchased a field and must go to examine it; I ask you, consider me excused." And another said, "I have purchased five yoke of oxen and am on my way to evaluate them; I ask you, consider me excused." And another said, "I have just married a woman, and therefore I cannot come."

The servant went and reported this to his master. Then the master of the house in a rage commanded his servant, "Go out quickly into the streets and alleys of the town and bring in here the poor and the crippled, the blind and the lame."

The servant reported, "Sir, your orders have been carried out and still there is room." The master then ordered the servant, "Go out to the highways and hedgerows and make people come in that my home may be filled. For, I tell you, none of those men who were invited will taste my dinner." [174]

---

[174] Luke 14:16-24

WEALTH & MATERIALISM, STATUS & PRESTIGE

As with all the commandments of God and the teachings of Jesus, there is a human benefit and a universal truth, not a capricious demand by a strict and angry God. As many university studies have shown, excessive wealth changes the way we think and feel toward other people.

Research is finding how significantly wealth impacts integrity, relations with others, and psychological health. Affluent kids are typically more anxious than lower-income children and are at higher risk for substance abuse, eating disorders, being deceptive, anxiety, depression, and committing theft.

Numerous studies have shown that wealth can also negatively affect empathy and kindness. Research has found that people at lower financial levels have more empathy than more affluent people and that wealthier test subjects behaved more aggressively and rudely.

Some studies suggest wealth itself does not cause discontent, but it is the perpetual pursuit of money and material possessions that causes unhappiness. Materialism is linked with less happiness in relationships and a higher susceptibility to addiction.

Teaching 144

No servant can serve two masters: for either he will hate the one and love the other; or else he will hold to the one and despise the other. You cannot serve God and wealth.

And the Pharisees also, who were covetous, heard all these things: and they derided him. And he said to them,

You are they which justify yourselves before men; but God knows your hearts: for that which is highly esteemed among men is abomination in the sight of God. [175]

---

[175] Luke 16:13-15

Teaching 145

Truly I say to you, Except you be changed, and become as little children, you will not enter into the Kingdom of Heaven.

Whosoever therefore will humble himself as this little child, the same is greatest in the Kingdom of Heaven. [176]

---

[176] Matthew 18: 3-4, Mark 9:35, Luke 9:48

Teaching 146

For everyone who exalts himself will be humbled, and whoever humbles himself will be exalted. [177]

---

[177] Matthew 23:11-12, Luke 14:11

Teaching 147

And behold, some are last who will be first, and some are first who will be last. [178]

Teaching 148

But woe to you that are rich! for you have received your reward.

Woe to you that are full! For you will hunger. Woe to you that laugh now! For you will mourn and weep.

Woe to you, when all men will speak well of you! for so did their fathers to the false prophets. [179]

---

[179] Luke 6:24-26

Teaching 149

A certain ruler asked him, saying, "Good Teacher, what will I do to inherit eternal life?" Jesus asked him,

Why do you call me good? No one is good, except one: God. You know the commandments: Don't commit adultery, Don't murder, Don't steal, Don't give false testimony, Honor your father and your mother.

He said, I have observed all these things from my youth up. When Jesus heard these things, he said to him,

You still lack one thing. Sell all that you have and distribute it to the poor. Then you will have treasure in heaven; then come, follow me.

But when he heard these things, he became very sad, for he was very rich. Jesus, seeing that he became very sad, said,

How hard it is for those who have riches to enter God's Kingdom! For it is easier for a rope to go through the eye of a needle than for a rich man to enter God's Kingdom. Children, how hard is it for them that trust in riches to enter the Kingdom of God! [180]

The Aramaic word Gamla means rope and camel. Native speakers would know the correct usage based on the context. The fact that the translator to the Greek used the wrong interpretation strongly indicates that there must have been an earlier version of the Gospels written in Aramaic and the Gospels were not written decades after Jesus lived, as put forward by current scholars.

---

[180] Matthew 19:23-24, Mark 10:23, Luke 18:18-24

Teaching 150

The Parable of the Rich Fool

And someone in the crowd said unto him, Master, speak to my brother, so that he divides the inheritance with me. And he said to him,

Man, who made me a judge or a divider over you?

And he said unto them,

Take heed and beware of covetousness: for a man's life consists not in the abundance of the things which he possesses.

And he spoke a parable unto them, saying,

The ground of a certain rich man brought
forth plentifully: And he thought to
himself, saying, "What should I do,
because I have no room where to bestow
my fruits?"

And he said, "I will do this: I will pull down
my barns and build greater; and there will I
bestow all my fruits and my goods."

And I will say to my soul, "Soul, you have
many goods laid up for many years; take
your ease, eat, drink, and be merry."

But God said unto him, "You fool, tonight
your soul will be required of you: then
whose will those things be, which you hast
provided?"

So is he who stores up treasure for himself and is not rich toward God. [181]

---

[181] Luke 12:13-21

Teaching 151

The Parable of the Rich Man and Lazarus

There was a certain rich man, who was clothed in purple and fine linen and fared sumptuously every day. And there was a certain beggar named Lazarus, who was laid at his gate, full of sores and desiring to be fed with the crumbs which fell from the rich man's table.

Moreover, the dogs came and licked his sores. And it came to pass that the beggar died and was carried by the angels into Abraham's bosom. The rich man also died and was buried.

And in hell, being in torment, he lifted up
his eyes and saw Abraham afar off and
Lazarus in his bosom. And he cried and
said, "Father Abraham, have mercy on me,
and send Lazarus that he may dip the tip
of his finger in water and cool my tongue;
for I am tormented in this flame."

But Abraham said, "Son, remember that
you in your lifetime received your good
things, and likewise Lazarus evil things; but
now he is comforted, and you are
tormented.

And besides all this, between us and you
there is a great gulf fixed, so that they who
would pass from here to you cannot;
neither can they pass to us, that would
come from there."

Then he said, "I pray you therefore, father, that you would send him to my father's house, for I have five brethren, that he may testify to them lest they also come into this place of torment." Abraham said to him, "They have Moses and the prophets; let them hear them."

And he said, "No, Father Abraham; but if one went to them from the dead, they will repent."

And he said to him, "If they don't hear Moses and the prophets, neither will they be persuaded by one risen from the dead." [182]

---

[182] Luke 16:19-31

Teaching 152

Then Jesus was led up by the Spirit into the wilderness to be tested by the devil. Again, the devil took him to an exceedingly high mountain, and showed him all the kingdoms of the world and their glory.

He said to him, "I will give you all of these things, if you will fall down and worship me." Then Jesus said to him,

Get behind me, Satan! For it is written, "You shall worship the Lord your God, and you shall serve him only." [183]

---

[183] Matthew 4:1, 8-10, Deuteronomy 6:13

Jesus on Religion

Hypocrites, False Prophets &
Blind Guides

One thing so many Christians and non-Christians alike do not realize about the teachings of Jesus is that he spoke out strongly against "organized religion" and its priestly class. Similarly, many of the academics and theologians of his day also received his condemnation. In this section are the largely forgotten and ignored teachings of Jesus—his teachings on false religion and its practitioners.

They make up a surprisingly large portion of his spoken words. There is much about Jesus even many Christians do not know because of how some church services are conducted and how post-Gospel writers are emphasized. There are in fact passages right there for all to see about Jesus that are rarely noticed, such as the role of women in following and financially supporting the works of Jesus and the disciples or the significant number of women that seem to have been around him continually.

The World of Jesus

This is not meant to be a history book, and I'm not qualified to give an exhaustive study of the history of the Israelites and their religion. However, a little background information will help put some of the situations depicted and the people into context, but even without these notes, I think the passages would stand on their own and the messages would be clear.

The religious landscape of the Israelites in the 1st century was in chaos, decay, and tumultuous change. There were ferocious divisions among numerous religious and political sects as Rabbinic Judaism grew in prominence even before the destruction of the Temple in 70 AD. To further add to the suffering of the people under occupation, religion had grown into a suffocating and burdensome system of rules and regulations that governed even the most minute details of life.

There were dictates for what foot should touch the ground first when getting out of bed in the morning, which shoe you should tie first, what prayers to say when going to the toilet, and strict discriminations against women and people suffering from illnesses, imperfections, and birth defects.

Jesus rejects many of the so-called laws of Moses (many of which were written hundreds of years after the death of Moses) with the words and spirit of his message, in favor of the laws of God. You will see here, as in the prior teachings, that Jesus defies and contradicts the supposed commandments of God in the Old Testament for killing and showing no mercy, taking an eye for an eye, swearing oaths, issuing curses, stealing the land of your enemies, ritually sacrificing animals, killing adulterers and those who violate the sabbath, and slaughtering women and children in war.

The Adversaries of Jesus

It is helpful to know the prime adversaries of Jesus in the Gospels: the Scribes, Pharisees, and Sadducees. Put simply, these were the religious scholars, preachers, priests, and theologians of their day. For a little more context, here is a brief description of their beliefs and roles in society.

Scribes—The scribes, also referred to as lawyers in the Gospels, were the educated and literate class, and it is said every village had at least one to fulfill legal and administrative duties in a society where most citizens could neither read nor write. Scribes were also experts in religious matters of Mosaic law and oral tradition, and many could have been either Sadducees or Pharisees.

Pharisees—The Pharisees were a religious-nationalist Jewish movement in the land of Israel during the Second Temple period. Pharisees claimed the authority of Moses in their interpretation of religious law and were well-regarded among the people as rabbis (spiritual teachers). After the destruction of the Second Temple in 70 AD, Pharisaic beliefs became the foundation of the form of Rabbinic Judaism that exists to this day.

Sadducees—The Sadducees, a word meaning "just" or "righteous" were an influential Jewish faction in Judea from the second century BC to the Roman destruction of the Temple in 70 AD. The Sadducees vied for prominence with other influential sects, principally the Pharisees and Essenes. The Sadducees put emphasis on the importance of the Temple with its rites and services, rather than Mosaic law.

Through collaboration with the Roman occupiers and by serving as their local administrators, the Sadducees were able to protect their wealth and influence and were among the aristocracy of Jewish society. They filled diverse political, administrative, and religious roles such as collecting the Temple tax, but were more concerned with earthly comfort and status than religious or political causes. They denied the resurrection of the body, or an afterlife, and largely left theology and nationalist ideas to the Pharisees.

Sanhedrin—Sanhedrin meaning "the assembly" or "council," was a tribunal of male elders in every city appointed to decide religious matters. During the Second Temple era, the Great Sanhedrin convened in the Temple in Jerusalem. The Romans recognized them as the authority in religious affairs. They are mentioned in the Gospels as the court of the High Priest that tried Jesus before his crucifixion. This 70-member supreme court in ancient Israel was composed of both Sadducees and Pharisees, but the chief priests as well as the high priest were Sadducees, and they composed most of the Sanhedrin.

Herodians—A group of powerful Jewish supporters of the Herodian dynasty which ruled various regions of the Levant as vassals of the Romans during Christ's time.

The Name "Jew" and the Antisemitism Issue
I hope you will see from the passages in this book that the Christian Bible does not teach antisemitism. Jesus was from the House of David and the Tribe of Judah, and his core disciples were Israelites.

The origin of the words *Jew*, *Jewish*, and *Judaism*, from Iudaismus, a Latinized version of an Ancient Greek word, is derived from the Hebrew Yehudah or "Judah." The broad terms Jew and Jewish encompassed not only religious customs and beliefs of the time, but the various cultural, ethnic, and national identities that often gave rise to conflict among themselves.

Judea, Samaria, and Idumea became the Roman province of Judaea after the son of the Idumean Herod the Great, Herod Archelaus, was replaced with a

Roman governor because of misrule and his unpopularity with the Jewish population. His brother Herod Antipas ruled Galilee as a Roman vassal. The Idumeans (or Edomites) were ethnic Arabs from what is modern-day Jordan who converted to Judaism around the year 100 BC. They comprised a large portion of the population of Judah in the time of Christ.

It should be evident—although no doubt made difficult by the complicated use of the word "Jew" in the region at the time, and the confusion passed down through the ages with its differing meanings and translations—that the enemies of Jesus were in the priestly class and among the pious religious leaders, not the Jewish people. Any apparent pejorative use of the word Jew was directed to the Judean Pharisees and scribes.

The Complete Jewish Bible [184] renders *Jews* as *Judeans* in the Gospels, which is probably more accurate than the KJV and most other translations that use Jews. The Gospel writers no doubt used the term Jew to differentiate them variously from Gentiles, as well as Galileans, Samaritans, Idumeans, and other followers of the God of Israel, who were often at odds with the Judeans. The Greek term *Ioudaios* was a term used by non-Jews originally referring to members of the southern Tribe of Judah specifically, and afterward the inhabitants of the former Kingdom of Judah and the Judean region as a whole.

---

[184] David H. Stern, Jewish New Testament Publications, 1998

The use of the word Jew in the Gospels can reasonably be viewed as a way for the authors to differentiate the various groups that followed the Mosaic religion and Judeans who considered themselves the only true Israelites. Clearly, the universally recognizable characters Jesus fought with still exist today in many forms across all religions and remain the adversaries of the Kingdom of God. You will see in the passages to follow patterns repeated among the religious leaders today—and not just in Christianity, but among all world religions.

The Church

Jesus never once said go to synagogue or church. "Church," by the way, means the global community of Christians, not a building. Jesus certainly didn't say to build a cathedral or a temple.

Nevertheless, reputable pastors, experienced teachers, and guided study are no doubt valuable to spiritual growth, but the greatest guide given to us by God according to Jesus are his words and the Holy Spirit, which he promised would guide those who studied his words.

Further good news is that you don't have to adopt the "praise and worship" culture or the admittedly sometimes cringe-worthy nature of certain aspects of "Churchianity," listen to Christian pop music, use tired catchphrases to describe your spirituality, dress a certain way, or even vote a certain way to draw value from the teachings of Jesus.

Implied in the teachings above is that it is important to continue learning and the church community writ large can help with that, as well as provide a support system to survive moments of doubt and suffering that we all endure. It is also a way for you to support others in their spiritual journey.

However, as a Paleo-Christian it is my belief that the physical church in all its forms should not be the center of your spiritual life, but the words of Jesus found in the Gospels. Trust your discernment and study of the scriptures. Be willing to grow and be patient with where others are on their spiritual journey. Realize you may have been wrong or misunderstood something in the past, and that all teachers, being human, can also make mistakes.

FALSE PROPHETS & BLIND GUIDES

Christianity, like Islam, Judaism, and all other world religions have become cultural edifices that have the tendency to impose an identity on their members. Like the "pearl of great price" or "treasure buried in a field," Jesus uses as a metaphor for the Kingdom of God, spiritual seekers must use their discernment and instincts to avoid the snares of false prophets and blind guides.

It must be said in no uncertain terms that what I have written in my commentary no way is meant to denigrate the underpaid and hardworking Christian clergy around the world who sacrifice their time, and increasingly their lives, in service to humanity and the furtherance of the message of Jesus.

Old Testament Christianity and the Church of Paul

Many Christians have handed over their exploration of the teachings of Jesus to church thought leaders. Likewise, non-Christians have deferred to academics, historians, and theologians to interpret Christ's message for them and are at the mercy of whatever is the current scholarship.

Equally alarming are the recent assertions, both overtly and subliminally, by Catholic and Protestant church leaders alike that you must go through them and accept their interpretations of the scriptures to get to God and any attempt by the uneducated masses to have a personal understanding of Jesus' teachings is dangerous.

A dictate that you need a priest or pastor steeped in a cult of personality with a special knowledge of the Bible to tell you what the scriptures demand, invariably by appealing to the writings of Paul and/or the Old Testament, is dangerously similar to what the Pharisees did in Jesus' time.

They might encourage you to "have a personal relationship with Christ," but bully you into accepting their interpretation of scripture, throwing in a host of Greek or Hebrew translations or harsh Mosaic laws if necessary. By insinuating that you can only get the truth from them they are directly contradicting what Jesus preached about guidance from the Holy Spirit.

Those who teach the primacy of religious leaders and the equality of post-Gospel writers with Jesus are taking a very similar path as the 1st century Pharisees who put forth that the Oral Tradition was equal to the Torah. Eventually, this led to the opinion that the Oral Tradition was superior to the Torah because it interpreted the law of Moses.

The Anti-Church

The False Prophets Jesus speaks of need not be religious leaders only. The message of Jesus is under assault from believers and nonbelievers alike from misguided or deceitful academics and theological thought leaders presenting distorted and intellectually dishonest interpretations of the scriptures to mislead people unfamiliar with the true words and their meaning.

Don't blindly fall into their trap, as it can be an endless swamp of esoteric terminology, antagonistic sensationalism to further their careers, and pseudo-historical conclusions about the "real" Jesus presented as fact.

You may also find that atheist and anti-Christian leaders display many of the arrogant, narrow-minded, and high-priest characteristics of the religious leaders in Jesus' time and today, prone to blindly accepting what an earlier academic said for fear of being ridiculed or shunned. You may find many anti-religious academics as smug in their belief system as the most objectionable preachers are in their righteousness.

Note also that many Pharisees agreed with Jesus but were afraid to acknowledge it for fear of retribution or losing their position in society.

Teaching 153

You blind guides, which strain at a gnat, and swallow a camel. [185]

The Scribes and Pharisees were able to accept complex regulations and convoluted theological concepts but unable to comprehend or perform the simplest, most basic spiritual concepts or moral and ethical principles.

---

[185] Matthhew 23:24

Teaching 154

Woe to you lawyers! For you took away the key of knowledge. You didn't enter in yourselves, and those who were entering in, you hindered. [186]

---

[186] Luke 11:52

Teaching 155

And why behold you the speck that is in your brother's eye, but realize not the beam that is in your own eye?

Or how can you say to your brother, "Brother, let me pull out the speck that is in your eye," when you yourself behold not the beam that is in your own eye?

You hypocrite! Cast out first the beam from your own eye, and then will you see more clearly to pull out the speck that is in your brother's eye. [187]

---

[187] Matthew 7:3-5, Luke 6:41-42

Teaching 156

Then one possessed by a demon, blind and mute, was brought to him; and he healed him, so that the blind and mute man both spoke and saw. All the multitudes were amazed, and said, "Can this be the son of David?" But when the Pharisees heard it, they said, "This man does not cast out demons except by Beelzebul, the prince of the demons."

Knowing their thoughts, Jesus said to them,

Every kingdom divided against itself is brought to desolation, and every city or house divided against itself will not stand. If Satan casts out Satan, he is divided against himself. How then will his kingdom stand?

If I by Beelzebul cast out demons, by whom do your children cast them out? Therefore, they will be your judges. But if I by the Spirit of God cast out demons, then God's Kingdom has come upon you.

Or how can one enter into the house of the strong man and plunder his goods, unless he first bind the strong man? Then he will plunder his house.

He who is not with me is against me, and he who doesn't gather with me, scatters.

Therefore, I tell you, every sin and blasphemy will be forgiven men, but the blasphemy against the Spirit will not be forgiven men.

Whoever speaks a word against the Son of Man, it will be forgiven him; but whoever speaks against the Holy Spirit, it will not be forgiven him, either in this age, or in that which is to come.

Either make the tree good and its fruit good or make the tree corrupt and its fruit corrupt; for the tree is known by its fruit.

You offspring of vipers, how can you, being evil, speak good things? For out of the abundance of the heart, the mouth speaks.

The good man out of his good treasure brings out good things, and the evil man out of his evil treasure brings out evil things.

I tell you that every foolish word that men speak, they will give account of it in the day of judgment. For by your words, you will be justified, and by your words you will be condemned.

Then certain of the scribes and Pharisees answered, "Teacher, we want to see a sign from you." But he answered them,

An evil and adulterous generation looks for a sign, but no sign will be given to it but the sign of Jonah the prophet. For as Jonah was three days and three nights in

the belly of the huge fish, so will the Son
of Man be three days and three nights in
the heart of the earth.

The men of Nineveh will stand up in the
judgment with this generation and will
condemn it, for they repented at the
preaching of Jonah; and behold, someone
greater than Jonah is here.

The Queen of the South will rise up in
the judgment with this generation and will
condemn it, for she came from the ends of
the earth to hear the wisdom of Solomon;
and behold, someone greater than
Solomon is here.

When an unclean spirit has gone out of a
man, he passes through waterless places

seeking rest, and doesn't find it. Then he says, "'I will return into my house from which I came;' and when he has come back, he finds it empty, swept, and put in order.

Then he goes and takes with himself seven other spirits more evil than he is, and they enter and dwell there. The last state of that man becomes worse than the first. Even so will it be also to this evil generation." [188]

---

[188] Matthew 12:22-45, Mark 3:22-26, Luke 11:14-20

Teaching 157

No servant can serve two masters: for either he will hate the one and love the other; or else he will hold to the one and despise the other. You cannot serve God and wealth.

And the Pharisees also, who were covetous, heard all these things: and they derided him. And he said to them,

You are they which justify yourselves before men; but God knows your hearts: for that which is highly esteemed among men is abomination in the sight of God. [189]

---

[189] Luke 16:13-15

Teaching 158

For justice I am come into this world, that they which see not might see; and that they which see might be made blind.

And some of the Pharisees which were with him heard these words, and said to him, Are we blind also? Jesus said to them,

If you were blind, you should have no sin: but now you say, "We see"; therefore, your sin remains. [190]

---

[190] John 9:39-41

Teaching 159

Woe to you, you blind guides, which say, Whoever will swear by the temple, it is nothing; but whoever will swear by the gold of the temple, he is a debtor!

You fools and blind: for which is greater, the gold, or the temple that sanctifies the gold?

And whoever will swear by the altar, it is nothing; but whoever swears by the gift that is upon it, he is guilty.

You fools and blind: for which is greater, the gift, or the altar that sanctifies the gift?

Who therefore will swear by the altar,
swears by it, and by all things on it.

And who will swear by the temple, swears
by it, and by him that dwells inside.

And he that will swear by heaven, swears
by the throne of God, and by him that sits
upon it. [191]

The Scribes and Pharisees put more emphasis and placed more value on the physical Temple building than what the Temple symbolized.

---

[191] Matthew 23:16-22

Teaching 160

The Parable of the Two Sons

But what do you think? A certain man had two sons; and he came to the first, and said, Son, go work today in my vineyard.

He answered and said, "I will not": but afterward he repented and went.

And he came to the second and said likewise. And he answered and said, "I go, sir": and went not.

Whether of the two did the will of his father?

(The chief priests and the elders) said unto him, "The first." Jesus said to them,

Truly I say to you, That the publicans and the prostitutes go into the Kingdom of God before you.

For John came unto you in the way of righteousness, and you believed him not: but the publicans and the prostitutes believed him: and you, when you had seen it, did not repent afterward, that you might believe him. [192]

---

[192] Matthew 21:28-32

Teaching 161

The Parable of the Vineyard Owner

Hear another parable: There was a certain householder, which planted a vineyard, and hedged it round about, and dug a winepress in it, and built a tower, and let it out to husbandmen, and went into a far country:

And when the time of the fruit drew near, he sent his servants to the husbandmen, that they might receive the fruits of it.

And the husbandmen took his servants, and beat one, and killed another, and stoned another.

Again, he sent other servants more than the first: and they did unto them likewise.

But last of all he sent unto them his son, saying, They will revere my son.

But when the husbandmen saw the son, they said among themselves, This is the heir; come, let us kill him, and let us seize on his inheritance.

And they caught him, and cast him out of the vineyard, and killed him.

When the lord of the vineyard comes, what will he do to those husbandmen?

They said unto him, He will miserably destroy those wicked men, and will rent out his vineyard to other husbandmen, which will give him the fruits in their seasons.

Jesus said to them,

Did you never read in the scriptures, "The stone which the builders rejected, the same is become the head of the corner: this is the Lord's doing, and it is marvelous in our eyes"?

Therefore, say I to you, The Kingdom of God will be taken from you, and given to a nation bringing forth the fruits of it.

And whosoever will fall on this stone will be broken but on whomever it will fall, it will grind him to powder.

And when the chief priests and Pharisees had heard his parables, they perceived that he spoke of them.

But when they sought to lay hands on him, they feared the multitude, because they took him for a prophet. [193]

---

[193] Matthew 21:33-44, Mark 12:1-11, Luke 20:9-18

Teaching 162

On that day Sadducees (those who say that there is no resurrection) came to him. They asked him, saying, "Teacher, Moses said, 'If a man dies, having no children, his brother shall marry his wife and raise up offspring for his brother.'

Now there were with us seven brothers. The first married and died, and having no offspring left his wife to his brother. In the same way, the second also, and the third, to the seventh.

After them all, the woman died. In the resurrection therefore, whose wife will she be of the seven? For they all had her."

But Jesus answered them,

You are mistaken, not knowing the scriptures, nor the power of God.

For in the resurrection, they neither marry nor are given in marriage, but are like God's angels in heaven.

But concerning the resurrection of the dead, haven't you read that which was spoken to you by God, saying, "I am the God of Abraham, and the God of Isaac, and the God of Jacob?"

God is not the God of the dead, but of the living. [194]

---

[194] Matthew 22:23-32

Teaching 163

And in them is fulfilled the prophecy of Isaiah, which said, "By hearing you will hear, and will not understand; and seeing you will see, and will not perceive:

For this people's heart is grown fat, and their ears are dull of hearing, and their eyes they have closed; lest at any time they should see with their eyes, and hear with their ears, and should understand with their heart, and should be converted, and I should heal them." [195]

---

[195] Matthew 13:14-15

Teaching 164

Then if anyone tells you, "Look, here is the Christ!" or, "Look, there!" don't believe it. For there will arise false Christs and false prophets, and will show signs and wonders, that they may lead astray, if possible, even the chosen ones. But you watch.

Behold, I have told you all things beforehand. [196]

---

[196] Matthew 24:24, Mark 13:22

Teaching 165

Not everyone who says to me, "Lord, Lord," will enter the Kingdom of Heaven, but he who does the will of my Father which is in heaven.

On that day many will say to me, 'Lord, Lord, did we not prophesy in your name, and cast out demons in your name, and do many mighty works in your name?'

And then will I declare to them, "I never knew you; depart from me, you evildoers." [197]

This makes it hard to believe that all non-Christians will go to hell if Jesus says those who do the will of God will enter the Kingdom of Heaven.

---

[197] Matthew 7:21-23

Teaching 166

And Jesus answered and said to them,

Take heed that no man deceives you.

For many will come in my name, saying, I am Christ; and will deceive many.

And many false prophets will rise and will deceive many.

For there will arise false Christs, and false prophets, and will show great signs and wonders; insomuch that, if it were possible, they will deceive the very elect. [198]

---

[198] Matthew 24:4-5, Matthew 24:11, Matthew 24:24, Mark 13:5-6, Luke 21:8

Teaching 167

He left them and departed. The disciples
came to the other side and had forgotten
to take bread. Jesus said to them,

Take heed and beware of the yeast of the
Pharisees and Sadducees.

They reasoned among themselves,
saying, "We brought no bread." Jesus,
perceiving it, said,

Why do you reason among yourselves, you
of little faith, because you have brought no
bread?

Don't you yet perceive or remember the
five loaves for the five thousand, and how
many baskets you took up, or the seven

loaves for the four thousand, and how many baskets you took up?

How is it that you don't perceive that I didn't speak to you concerning bread? But beware of the yeast of the Pharisees and Sadducees.

Then they understood that he didn't tell them to beware of the yeast of bread, but of the teaching of the Pharisees and Sadducees. [199]

---

[199] Matthew 16:5-12, Mark 8:13-16

Teaching 168

Most certainly, I tell you, one who doesn't enter by the door into the sheep fold, but climbs up some other way, is a thief and a robber.

But one who enters in by the door is the shepherd of the sheep. The gatekeeper opens the gate for him, and the sheep listen to his voice. He calls his own sheep by name and leads them out.

Whenever he brings out his own sheep, he goes before them, and the sheep follow him, for they know his voice. They will by no means follow a stranger but will flee from him; for they don't know the voice of strangers.

Most certainly, I tell you, I am the sheep's
door. All who came before me are thieves
and robbers, but the sheep didn't listen to
them. I am the door. If anyone enters in by
me, he will be saved, and will go in and go
out, and will find pasture.

The thief only comes to steal, kill, and
destroy. I came that they may have life and
may have it abundantly.

I am the good shepherd. The good
shepherd lays down his life for the sheep.
He who is a hired hand, and not a
shepherd, who doesn't own the sheep,
sees the wolf coming, leaves the sheep, and
flees.

The wolf snatches the sheep and scatters them. The hired hand flees because he is a hired hand and doesn't care for the sheep. I am the good shepherd.

I know my own, and I'm known by my own; even as the Father knows me, and I know the Father.

I lay down my life for the sheep. I have other sheep, which are not of this fold. I must bring them also, and they will hear my voice. They will become one flock with one shepherd. [200]

---

[200] John 10:1-16

HYPOCRISY &
SELF-RIGHTEOUSNESS

In the following passages, you will see how Jesus puts a premium on humility and self-awareness of our personal failings and despises religious hypocrisy and entitlement of the religious elite. Passages like these were some of the most exciting to me as a child as it showed Jesus, not as a weak pushover, but as a strong and courageous fighter against the truly deceitful, wicked, and inherently evil forces in this world.

Teaching 169

You are those who justify yourselves
before men, but God knows your hearts;
for what is exalted among men is an
abomination in the sight of God. [201]

---

[201] Luke 16:15

Teaching 170

The Parable of the Pharisee
and the Tax Collector

He also spoke this parable to certain people who were convinced of their own righteousness, and who despised all others.

Two men went up into the temple to pray; one was a Pharisee, and the other was a tax collector. The Pharisee stood and prayed to himself like this: "God, I thank you that I am not like the rest of men, extortionists, unrighteous, adulterers, or even like this tax collector. I fast twice a week. I give tithes of all that I get."

But the tax collector, standing far away, wouldn't even lift up his eyes to heaven, but beat his breast, saying, "God, be merciful to me, a sinner!"

I tell you; this man went down to his house justified rather than the other; for everyone who exalts himself will be humbled, but he who humbles himself will be exalted. [202]

---

[202] Luke 18:9-14

Teaching 171

Beware you of the leaven of the
Pharisees, which is hypocrisy.

For there is nothing covered, that will not
be revealed; neither hid, that will not be
known.

Therefore, whatever you have spoken in
darkness will be heard in the light; and that
which you have spoken in the ear in closets
will be proclaimed upon the housetops.

And I say to you my friends, Be not afraid
of them that kill the body, and after that
have no more that they can do.

But I will forewarn you whom you will fear:
Fear him, which after he has killed has
power to cast into hell; yes, I say to you,
Fear him. [203]

---

[203] Luke 12:1-5

Teaching 172

Then the Pharisees went and took counsel how they might entrap him in his talk.

They sent their disciples to him, along with the Herodians, saying, "Teacher, we know that you are honest, and teach the way of God in truth, no matter whom you teach; for you aren't partial to anyone.

Tell us therefore, what do you think? Is it lawful to pay taxes to Caesar, or not?" But Jesus perceived their wickedness, and said,

Why do you test me, you hypocrites? Show me the tax money."

They brought him a denarius. He asked them,

Whose is this image and inscription?

They said to him, "Caesar's." Then, he said to them,

Give therefore to Caesar the things that are Caesar's, and to God the things that are God's.

When they heard it, they marveled, and left him and went away. [204]

Here we see the distinction Jesus made between the spiritual world and the earthly political world for those who would hope for a theocracy to rule on the earth.

---

[204] Matthew 22:15-22, Mark 12:13-17, Luke 20:20-26

Teaching 173

But woe to you, scribes and Pharisees, hypocrites! for you shut up the Kingdom of Heaven against men: for you neither go in yourselves, neither allow you them that are entering to go in.

Woe to you, scribes and Pharisees, hypocrites! for you compass sea and land to make one convert, and when he is made, you make him twofold more the child of hell than yourselves. [205]

Jesus is speaking here of the attempts by the scribes and Pharisees to convert the children of Israel to their ideas that placed primacy on the "traditions" of the Oral Torah and their false doctrines. Their converts are therefore even more misguided and misinformed than themselves, he says.

---

[205] Matthew 23: 13,15

RELIGIOUS STATUS & THE OUTWARDLY RELIGIOUS

Jesus preached his message not only before the well-educated professional experts in the philosophy and religious teachings of the day, who largely rejected him, but to the outcasts, poor, illiterate, second-class citizens, and misfits of society who followed him in droves.

In short, his message does not have to be conveyed by theologians, academics, or priests, and the elite in his Kingdom are the humble and lower class. A significant number of the verses in the Gospels relating the spoken words of Jesus deal harshly with the outwardly religious and the religious leaders of his time. The profoundness of this focus of Jesus' animosity cannot be understated.

As you might imagine, this major emphasis among his teachings is not a central focus of Christian leaders, church liturgy, or many practicing Christians, who have been misdirected elsewhere. As with many of Jesus' attacks against the religious leaders of his time, parallels can be seen today, not only among Christianity and Judaism but in all the world's religions, in their efforts to cast themselves as the new "Chosen People" with the exclusive ownership of God.

Teaching 174

But don't be called Rabbi: for one is your Master, even Christ (the Messiah); and all you are brothers.

And call no man your father upon the earth: for one is your Father, who is in heaven. Neither be you called leaders: for one is your Leader, even Christ. [206]

In the *KJV* this reads "Master" instead of the Aramaic translation "Leader."

---

[206] Matthew 23:8-10

Teaching 175

Woe to you Pharisees! for you love the best seat in the synagogues and salutations in the marketplaces.

Woe to you! for you are like graves which are not seen, and men walk over them without knowing it. [207]

Jesus is implying that the false teachings of the Pharisees are like unmarked graves people do not see and by encountering them become unclean, impure, and corrupted by being exposed to them. It might also imply that, like an unseen open grave, unsuspecting converts might unwittingly fall into their deception.

---

[207] Luke 11:43-44

Teaching 176

Who then is the faithful and wise servant, whom his lord has set over his household, to give them their food in due season?

Blessed is that servant whom his lord finds doing so when he comes. Most certainly I tell you that he will set him over all that he has.

But if that evil servant should say in his heart, "my lord is delaying his coming," and begins to beat his fellow servants, and eat and drink with the drunkards, the lord of that servant will come in a day when he doesn't expect it and, in an hour, when he doesn't know it, and will cut him in pieces and appoint his portion with the

hypocrites.

That is where the weeping and grinding of
teeth will be. [208]

This teaching addresses the outwardly religious who
profess to be followers of God but think that they can
get away with the mistreatment of their fellow citizens
because they think death and the day of judgment is
far off or that they can repent at a later date. But Jesus
warns that the day of judgment could come anytime
without warning. A similar theme of spiritual
preparedness can be found in the *Parable of the Ten
Virgins.* [209]

---

[208] Matthew 24:42-51, Mark 13:34-37, Luke 12:35-48
[209] Matthew 25:1–13

Teaching 177

Woe to you, scribes and Pharisees, hypocrites! You clean the outside of the cup and of the platter, but inside they are full of extortion and excess.

You blind Pharisee, first cleanse that which is within the cup and platter, that the outside of them may be clean also.

Woe to you, scribes and Pharisees, hypocrites! for you are like whitewashed tombs, which indeed appear beautiful outside, but inside are full of dead men's bones, and of all uncleanness.

Even so you also outwardly appear righteous to men, but within you are full of hypocrisy and iniquity.[210]

---

[210] Matthew 23:25-28

Teaching 178

Woe unto you, scribes and Pharisees, hypocrites! because you build the tombs of the prophets, and garnish the tombs of the righteous,

And say, If we had been in the days of our fathers, we would not have been partakers with them in the blood of the prophets.

Wherefore you are witnesses unto yourselves, that you are the children of them which killed the prophets.

Fill you up then the measure of your fathers.

You serpents, you generation of vipers, how can you escape the damnation of hell?

Wherefore, behold, I send unto you prophets, and wise men, and scribes: and some of them you will kill and crucify; and some of them will you scourge in your synagogues, and persecute them from city to city:

That upon you may come all the righteous blood shed upon the earth, from the blood of righteous Abel unto the blood of Zacharias son of Barachias, whom you slew between the temple and the altar.

Truly I say unto you, All these things will come upon this generation.

Oh Jerusalem, Jerusalem, you that kills the prophets, and stones them which are sent to you, how often would I have gathered thy children together, even as a hen gathers her chickens under her wings, and you would not![211]

---

[211] Matthew 23:29-37, Luke 11:47

Teaching 179

Why do you call me, "Lord, Lord," and don't do the things which I say?[212]

Teaching 180

Everyone who comes to me, and hears my words, and does them, I will show you who he is like.

He is like a man building a house, who dug and went deep, and laid a foundation on the rock. When a flood arose, the stream broke against that house, and could not shake it, because it was founded on the rock.

But he who hears, and doesn't do, is like a man who built a house on the earth without a foundation, against which the stream broke, and immediately it fell, and the ruin of that house was great. [213]

---

[213] Luke 6:47-49

Teaching 181

And it came to pass, that he went through the grain fields on the sabbath day; and his disciples began, as they went, to pluck the ears of grain. And the Pharisees said unto him, Behold, why do they on the sabbath day that which is not lawful? And he said unto them,

Have you never read what David did, when he had need, and was hungry, he, and they that were with him?

How he went into the house of God in the days of Abiathar the high priest, and ate the shewbread, which is not lawful to eat but for the priests, and gave also to them which were with him?

And he said unto them,

The sabbath was made for man, and not man for the sabbath: Therefore, the Son of Man is Lord also of the sabbath. [214]

With one simple revolutionary phrase—"the Sabbath was made for man; man was not made for the Sabbath"—Jesus nullifies 99% of the concepts and rationales for a highly structured, strict, and hierarchical religion.

This scenario is repeated elsewhere where the cold-hearted religious authorities accuse Jesus, and even a man that he healed, of breaking the strict laws of working on the sabbath because they are more concerned with obeying rules (and control of the people) than they are with compassion, mercy, and witnessing the power of God.

---

[214] Matthew 12:1-8, Mark 2:23-28. Luke 6:1-5

VAIN RELIGION & EMPTY WORSHIP

There is an ongoing debate on whether Jesus intended to merely supplement Judaism or to start a new religion. It seems clear from reading his words that perhaps Jesus came to do neither, but something more radical—a concept as revolutionary 2,000 years ago as it is today.

Jesus intended to start a spiritual revolution with a chance at personal transformation that frees humanity from the burden of dead religion. True religion transcends "faith traditions." These universal truths exist beyond doctrine, ritual, and observance of ceremony and custom.

The key takeaways from what Jesus said about religion are:

- Religious practice was created for humanity; humanity wasn't created for religion. You don't have to be the slave of your religion.
- You don't need a priestly class between you and God. In fact, they can keep you from God.
- Following Jesus requires little.
- God doesn't want groveling, fearful worship, and painful sacrifice, but love, mercy, and service to your fellow humans.

- Spirituality should be simple, not rigid, complex, and legalistic.
- Spirituality and religious practice should be outwardly focused on serving humanity and sharing the Good News, not just inward looking.

Jesus didn't tell us everything or prescribe rules for every possible scenario in life—the religion of his day did that, and it was bondage. Jesus expected his followers to use their brains and their hearts based on some very simple principles for guidance, e.g., let those with ears to hear and eyes to see know the truth.

Teaching 182

Then the Pharisees and some of the scribes gathered together to him, having come from Jerusalem. Now when they saw some of his disciples eating bread with defiled, that is unwashed, hands, they found fault.

The Pharisees and the scribes asked him, "Why don't your disciples walk according to the tradition of the elders, but eat their bread with unwashed hands?"

He answered them,

Well did Isaiah prophesy of you hypocrites, as it is written, "This people honors me with their lips, but their heart is far from me. But they worship me in vain, teaching as doctrines the commandments of men." For you set aside the commandment of God and hold tightly to the tradition of men—the washing of pitchers and cups, and you do many other such things.

He said to them,

Full well do you reject the commandment of God, that you may keep your tradition.[215]

Jesus is speaking here of the traditions of the Oral Torah espoused by the Pharisees, which grew to be the cornerstone of Rabbinic Judaism, but you can easily see parallels in Christianity over the centuries as church law and doctrine displaced Christ's teachings.

---

[215] Matthew 15:1-9, Mark 7:1-2, 5-9, Isaiah 29:13

Teaching 183

While Jesus was speaking to the multitudes, behold, his mother and his brothers *stood* outside, seeking to speak to him. One said to him, "Behold, your mother and your brothers stand outside, seeking to speak to you."

But he answered him who spoke to him,

Who is my mother? Who are my brothers?

He stretched out his hand toward his disciples, and said,

Behold, my mother and my brothers! For whoever does the will of my Father who is in heaven, he is my brother, and sister, and mother. [216]

---

[216] Matthew 12:46-50, Mark 31-35

Teaching 184

No one puts a new piece of cloth on an old garment; for the patch would tear away from the garment, and a worse hole is made.

Neither do people put new wine into old wine skins, or else the skins would burst, and the wine be spilled, and the skins ruined.

No, they put new wine into fresh wine skins, and both are preserved. [217]

The new wine is Jesus' message and ministry, and the new wine skins his followers. The old wine is the religion of the past and the old wine skins those who cling to it.

---

[217] Matthew 9:16-17, Mark 2:22, Luke 5:37-38

Teaching 185

I tell you that many will come from the east and the west, and will sit down with Abraham, Isaac, and Jacob in the Kingdom of Heaven, but the children of the Kingdom will be thrown out into the outer darkness. There will be weeping and gnashing of teeth." [218]

All races, sexes, and ethnic groups will be welcome in the new Kingdom that is arriving, but those who cling to dead religious ritual and tradition will be excluded.

---

[218] Matthew 8:11-12

Teaching 186

Woe to you, scribes and Pharisees, hypocrites! For you tithe mint, dill, and cumin, and have left undone the weightier matters of the law: justice, mercy, and faith. But you ought to have done these, and not to have left the other undone.[219]

Here again, Jesus shows "the law" as not being merely the books of the Torah and its endless restrictions on everything from gathering sticks on the sabbath to eating shellfish, but the more important things such as justice, mercy, and faith. Clearly, these seem to be the things he was referring to when he said the law would be fulfilled by his kingdom.

---

[219] Matthew 23:23, Luke 11:42

Teaching 187

You are of your father the devil, and the lusts of your father you will do. he was a murderer from the beginning, and abode not in the truth, because there is no truth in him. When he speaks a lie, he speaks of his own: for he is a liar, and the father of it.

And because I tell you the truth, you believe me not. Which of you convicts me of sin?

And if I say the truth, why do you not believe me? He that is of God hears God's words: you therefore hear them not, because you are not of God.

Then answered the Judeans, and said to him, "Don't we correctly say that you are a Samaritan, and have a devil?" Jesus answered,

I do not have a devil; but I honor my Father, and you dishonor me. And I don't seek my own glory: there is one who seeks and judges.

Truly, Truly, I say to you, If a man keeps my sayings, he will never see death.

Then said the Judeans to him, "Now we know that you have a devil. Abraham is dead, and the prophets; and you say, If a man keep my saying, he will never taste of death. Are you greater than our father Abraham, which is dead? And the prophets are dead: who do you think you are?" Jesus answered,

If I honor myself, my honor is nothing: it is
my Father that honors me; of whom you
say, that he is your God: Yet you have not
known him; but I know him: and if I should
say, I know him not, I will be a liar like you:
but I know him and keep his saying.

Your father Abraham rejoiced to see my
day: and he saw it and was glad.

Then said the Judeans to him, "You are
not yet fifty years old, and have you seen
Abraham?" Jesus said to them,

Truly, Truly, I say to you, Before
Abraham was, I am.

Then took they up stones to cast at him:
but Jesus hid himself, and went out of

the temple, going through the midst of
them, and so passed by. [220]

---

[220] John 8:44-59

Teaching 188

Jesus said to them,

Did you never read in the scriptures, "The stone which the builders rejected, the same is become the head of the corner: this is the Lord's doing, and it is marvelous in our eyes"?

Therefore, say I to you, The Kingdom of God will be taken from you, and given to a nation bringing forth the fruits thereof. And whoever falls on this stone will be broken but on whomsoever it will fall, it will grind him to powder.

And when the chief priests and Pharisees had heard his parables, they realized that he spoke of them.

But when they sought to lay hands on him, they feared the multitude, because they took him for a prophet. [221]

---

[221] Matthew 21:42-46

Teaching 189

The Pharisees and Sadducees came, and testing him, asked him to show them a sign from heaven. But he answered them,

When it is evening, you say, "It will be fair
weather, for the sky is red."

In the morning, "It will be foul weather
today, for the sky is red and threatening."
Hypocrites! You know how to discern the
appearance of the sky, but you can't
discern the signs of the times!

An evil and adulterous generation seeks
after a sign, and there will be no sign given

to it, except the sign of the prophet Jonah. [222]

The sign of the prophet is a reference to Jonah being in the belly of the whale for three days, a foretelling of Christ's death and resurrection. It also carries an ominous warning to the Pharisees and Sadducees that the hated Gentiles in Nineveh repented but you and those like you will not.

In *Gospel Light* by Dr. George M. Lamsa (Aramaic Bible Society, 1999) he states that to be "in the belly of a whale," as Jonah was in the Bible story, is a well-known Aramaic idiom for profound depression and not to be taken literally.

---

[222] Matthew 16:1-4, Matthew 12:39, Mark 8:11-12, Luke 11:29-30.

Teaching 190

The Pharisees therefore said to him, "You bear witness of Yourself; Your witness is not true." Jesus answered and said to them,

Even if I bear witness of myself, my witness is true, for I know where I came from and where I am going; but you do not know where I come from and where I am going. You judge according to the flesh; I judge no one.

And yet if I do judge, my judgment is true; for I am not alone, but I am with the Father who sent me.

It is also written in your law that the testimony of two men is true. I am One who bears witness of myself, and the Father who sent me bears witness of me.

Then they said to him, "Where is Your Father?" Jesus answered,

You know neither me nor my Father. If you had known me, you would have known my Father also.

These words Jesus spoke in the treasury, as He taught in the temple; and no one laid hands on him, for his time had not yet come. [223]

---

[223] John 8:13-20

Teaching 191

For I say to you, that except your righteousness exceeds the righteousness of the scribes and Pharisees, you will in no way enter the Kingdom of Heaven.[224]

---

[224] Matthew 5:20

Teaching 192

Either the tree is good, and its fruit is good; or else the tree is corrupt, and its fruit is corrupt: for the tree is known by its fruit.

Oh, generation of vipers, how can you, being evil, speak good things? For out of the abundance of the heart the mouth speaks.

A good man out of the good treasure of the heart brings forth good things: and an evil man out of the evil treasure brings forth evil things.[225]

---

[225] Matthew 12:33-35

Teaching 193

Search the scriptures; for in them you think you have eternal life: and they are they which testify of me.

And you will not come to me, that you might have life.

I receive not honor from men. But I know you, that you have not the love of God in you.

I have come in my Father's name, and you receive me not: if another will come in his own name, him you will receive. [226]

---

[226] John 5:39-43

Teaching 194

And they came to Jerusalem: and Jesus went into the temple and began to cast out them that sold and bought in the temple, and overthrew the tables of the moneychangers, and the seats of them that sold doves; And would not allow any man to carry any vessel through the temple. And he taught, saying to them,

Is it not written; "My house will be called of all nations the house of prayer?" but you have made it a den of thieves.

And the scribes and chief priests heard it and sought how they might destroy him: for they feared him, because all the people were astonished at his doctrine. [227]

---

[227] Matthew 21:11-13, Mark 11:15-18, Luke 19:45, Isaiah 56:7

The Temple priests required that monetary donations made by pilgrims to "Herod's" Temple could not be made in their own Greek or Roman currency, but in the approved coinage of shekels or tetradrachms, so they had to be exchanged at unfair rates. Likewise, animals for sacrifice were sold at exorbitant prices. This was particularly hard on women and the poor who could often only afford a simple dove to offer for sacrifice.

The outer Temple courtyard or Court of the Gentiles had become a boisterous market filled with vendors, money changers, and a menagerie of animals sold for sacrifice. Because observant Jews were required to make pilgrimages to the Temple, this bazaar became big business for the priests, who collected Temple taxes and profited from the offerings, making them extremely wealthy. The children of Israel in the Levant and the diaspora (except the priests of course) were also required to pay Temple taxes, furthering the riches of the priestly class.

Teaching 195

No servant can serve two masters: for either he will hate the one and love the other; or else he will hold to the one and despise the other. You cannot serve God and wealth.

And the Pharisees also, who were lovers of money, heard all these things: and they derided him. And he said to them,

You are they which justify yourselves before men; but God knows your hearts: for that which is highly esteemed among men is abomination in the sight of God. [228]

---

[228] Luke 16:13-15

Teaching 196

Beware of false prophets, which come to you in sheep's clothing, but inwardly they are ravening wolves.

You will know them by their fruits.

Do men gather grapes of thorns, or figs of thistles?

Even so, every good tree brings forth good fruit; but a corrupt tree brings forth evil fruit.

A good tree cannot bring forth evil fruit, neither can a corrupt tree bring forth good fruit.

Every tree that brings not forth good fruit is hewn down and cast into the fire.

Wherefore by their fruits you will know them. [229]

Many Christian leaders insist that salvation is by faith and God's grace alone and not by "works." True, but the two are not exclusive of each other, and outward behavior gives evidence of your inner soul.

Here again, Jesus makes clear that your actions are inextricably linked with any claims to salvation, righteousness, and especially any claims to be a teacher of God. The relentless attempt to reduce the Jesus message to legalistic bullet points destroys their complexity and subtlety.

---

[229] Matthew 7:15-20

Teaching 197

How can you believe, which receive honor
one of another, and seek not the honor
that comes from God only?

Do not think that I will accuse you to the
Father: there is one that accuses you,
even Moses, in whom you trust.

For had you believed Moses, you would
have believed me: for he wrote of me. But
if you believe not his writings, how will you
believe my words? [230]

---

[230] John 5:44-47

Teaching 198

Then spoke Jesus to the multitude, and
to his disciples, saying,

The scribes and the Pharisees sit in
Moses' seat: All therefore whatever they
bid you observe, that observe and do; but
do not you after their works: for they say,
and do not.

For they bind heavy burdens and grievous
to bear and lay them on men's shoulders;
but they themselves will not lift them with
one of their fingers.

But all their works they do to be seen by
men: they make broad their phylacteries,
and enlarge the borders of their garments,

and love the uppermost rooms at feasts, and the chief seats in the synagogues, and greetings in the markets, and to be called of men, "Rabbi, Rabbi."[231]

---

[231] Matthew 23:1-7

Teaching 199

Take heed that you do not your offerings before men, to be seen of them: otherwise, you have no reward of your Father who is in heaven.

Therefore, when you do your offerings, do not sound a trumpet before you, as the hypocrites do in the synagogues and in the streets, that they may have glory of men.

Truly I say to you, They have their reward. But when you do offerings, let not your left hand know what your right hand does that your alms may be in secret: and your Father who sees in secret himself will reward you openly. [232]

---

[232] Matthew 6:1-4

Teaching 200

And when you pray, do not be as the hypocrites are because they love to pray standing in the synagogues and in the corners of the streets, that they may be seen of men.

Truly I say to you, they have their reward. But you, when you pray, go into your closet, and when you have shut your door, pray to your Father who is in secret; and your Father who sees in secret will reward you openly. [233]

---

[233] Matthew 6:5-6

Teaching 201

They answered him, We are Abraham's seed, and were never in bondage to any man: how say you, You will be made free? Jesus answered them,

Truly, Truly, I say to you, Whoever commits sin is the servant of sin. And the servant abides not in the house for ever: but the Son abides ever.

If the Son therefore will make you free, you will be free indeed. I know that you are Abraham's seed; but you seek to kill me, because my word has no place in you.

I speak that which I have seen with my Father: and you do that which you have seen with your father.

They answered and said to him,
Abraham is our father. Jesus said to
them,

If you were Abraham's children, you would
do the works of Abraham.

But now you seek to kill me, a man that has
told you the truth, which I have heard of
God: this did not Abraham. You do the
deeds of your father.

Then said they to him, We be not born of
fornication; we have one Father, even
God. Jesus said to them,

If God were your Father, you would love
me: for I proceeded forth and came from
God; neither came I of myself, but he sent
me.

Why do you not understand my speech? Even because you cannot hear my word. [234]

---

[234] John 8:33-43

Teaching 202

And when he had called all the people to him, he said to them,

Listen to me every one of you and understand: There is nothing from without a man, that entering into him can defile him: but the things which come out of him, those are they that defile the man. If any man have ears to hear, let him hear.

And when he was entered into the house from the people, his disciples asked him concerning the parable. And he said to them,

Are you so without understanding also? Do you not perceive that whatever thing from without enters the man, it cannot defile him; Because it enters not into his heart, but into the belly, and goes out into the draught, purging all food?

And he said,

That which comes from out of the man, that defiles the man. For from within, out of the heart of men, proceed evil thoughts, adulteries, fornications, murders, thefts, covetousness, wickedness, deceit, lasciviousness, an evil eye, blasphemy, pride, foolishness: All these evil things come from within, and defile the man. [235]

This pronouncement would obviously be against "the Law," so Jesus clearly is not referring to strict dietary and other oppressive commandments of the Torah. When he says "not one jot or tittle" of the law should

---

[235] Mark 7:14-23, [235] Matthew 15:10-20

be violated clearly seems to refer to the superior law of God, which he explains several times elsewhere, which is love of God and others as much as you love yourself, as well as justice, mercy, and charity.

CONCLUSION: WHAT NOW?

If you find value in these teachings and they ring true to you, please continue your search, and learn as much as you feel compelled to do. I expect you saw in these teachings an Outcasts Manifesto beneficial to your spiritual journey, as well as things that are helpful in dispelling myths and misconceptions about Jesus.

As I wrote in the Introduction, this is not an exhaustive study of the Christian Bible, but a primer of the Gospels. There are other things Jesus said and did worthy of further study. I did not include miracles or prophecies but there are extremely useful insights included in them, although I would not get drawn into the temptation of focusing on prophecy in your early months or even years of study. There is a lucrative "Prophecy Industrial Complex" out there, much of which is little more than Apocalypse entertainment and nothing else. Focus on the complete Gospels, then the New Testament.

I hope you also saw in these teachings that Jesus never said, "Worship me or I'll condemn you to Hell for all eternity." He certainly never said, "You must have a church or a priestly class to control your understanding of me." I also trust the knowledge of his words will give you the tools to sense when there is an agenda among his detractors, as well as attempts by various forms of New Age Christianity or advocates of the Prosperity Gospel to depict Christianity in ways that don't ring true to you.

There is an old adage that says, "If you ask four people a question you will get five opinions." Two people can interpret the same scripture completely differently. No human can know the whole truth and no religious leader has all the answers or can confine God to a narrow box or tell you what God thinks. Beware of opinion being presented as fact and observe the early Church wisdom of not destroying all the new Christian converts' traditions and culture.

I also hope you sense, as many now do, that the world needs a spiritual revolution, particularly within the church. In my humble opinion, as with the printing of *The Gutenberg Bible* which allowed the common people to read and interpret the Bible for themselves, that only by returning to the Paleo-Christian roots of Jesus' teachings can we hope to avoid being squeezed between the old declining, quasi-pagan, ritual-bound church and faddish New Age cults of self-help pop psychology Christianity, the Prosperity Gospel or even worse, warmongering apocalyptic political Christianity.

The ultimate question, however, is in the dilemma the legendary Christian writer and former atheist and former occultist C.S. Lewis presented. Either Jesus was a liar, a lunatic, or he told the truth. I hope the teachings included in this book help you answer that question.

BIBLIOGRAPHY & RECOMMENDED READING

Holy Bible: From the Ancient Eastern Text: George M. Lamsa's Translation From the Aramaic of the Peshitta, Harper & Row; 37946th edition (May 8, 1985)

The Holy Bible, King James Authorized Version, Public Domain.

The World English Bible™ (WEB), by Public Domain.

Gospel Light: A Revised Annotated Edition by George M. Lamsa (Author), Janet Magiera (Editor), The Aramaic Bible Society, Inc.; Annotated edition (July 1, 2002)

Idioms in the Bible Explained and a Key to the Original Gospels by George M. Lamsa, HarperCollins; Reprint edition (October 23, 1985)

Women Remembered: Jesus' Female Disciples, by Joan Taylor and Helen Bond, Hodder Faith (August 29, 2023)

The Zen Teachings of Jesus by Kenneth S. Leong, Crossroad; Expanded, Subsequent edition (March 1, 2001)

The Lost Gospel Q: The Original Sayings of Jesus by Marcus Borg (Author), Thomas Moore (Introduction), Ulysses Press; First Trade Paper edition (March 4, 2022)

The Logia of Yeshua: The Sayings of Jesus by Guy Davenport, Counterpoint (June 1, 1998)

Bible Gateway https://www.biblegateway.com/

Misrepresenting Jesus: Debunking Bart D. Ehrman's "Misquoting Jesus" by Edward D. Andrews, Christian Publishing House (October 2, 2019)

How Christianity Changed the World by Alvin J. Schmidt, Zondervan (December 12, 2004)

Fabricating Jesus: How Modern Scholars Distort the Gospels by Craig A. Evans, IVP Books; Expanded edition (October 31, 2006)

Rabbinic Judaism Debunked: Debunking the Myth of Rabbinic Oral Law by Eitan Bar and Golan Broshi, independently published (February 4, 2019)

Complete Jewish Bible: An English Version by David H. Stern, Lederer Messianic Publications (June 1, 1998)

The Catholic Bible, Personal Study Edition: New American Bible by Jean Marie Heisberger, Oxford University Press (May 11, 1995)

Synopsis of the Four Gospels by Kurt Aland (Editor), Fortress Press; 1st Revised edition (January 1, 1985)

Palestine in the Time of Christ by Edmond Stapfer, DD, Annie Harwood Holmden (translator), Hodder and Stoughton (1886)

Daily Life in Palestine at the Time of Christ Paperback by H. Daniel-Rops, Phoenix Press (2002)

The New Greek-English Interlinear New Testament, Tyndale House Publishers, Inc.; 3rd edition (October 2, 1990)

Life Application Study Bible, New American Standard Bible—Updated Edition, Zondervan (January 1, 2000

Yeshua Speaks

www.ingramcontent.com/pod-product-compliance
Lightning Source LLC
Chambersburg PA
CBHW071403090426
42737CB00011B/1336